The Power of Mentalizing

Foreword

It is an honour to be asked to write a foreword to this book. There is a pressing need for mentalizing to be explained clearly and in plain language if it is to be useful to interested people in their work and everyday life. Putting aside the term *mentalizing* for a moment, it seems obvious to us all that we, as human beings, are efficient at 'reading' our own and others minds and we expect others to 'read' ours reasonably accurately. If we could not do this for ourselves and do it with others, effective social interaction would grind to a halt. Using this unique human ability of being sensitive to mind states, we are able to piece together why we do what we do and what motivates others; we gain a mental picture of who we are and who others are and how we and they feel at any given time; we are the same person in the past as we are in the present; we place ourselves in a personal narrative over time; when interacting with others we have a comfortable to and from, serve and return process that moves along smoothly and we can 'jointly see to things' together as we generate mutual understanding. We feel that we are part of a group. We are so good at this process that most of the time we are not aware we are doing it. This whole complex process has been given this ungainly name—mentalizing—the subject of this book. So what is it?

When explaining mentalizing to interested people as the overall process through which we understand that mind states determine actions, their natural reaction is to say 'of course, that is obvious'. Indeed, it seems so apparent that we may not think about it further and simply file mentalizing in our own mind as part of psychobabble or folk psychology. It is only when looked at in more detail that the whole idea of social interaction and how we understand ourselves and each other, becomes more difficult to grasp. Mental states lack physical substance and are invisible to others but, of course, despite being intangible, they can have very real consequences through their power to direct action. Human beliefs are determinants of behaviour with massive observable consequences; for that reason, they are in many ways of far greater significance than the physical world with which they have only a loose relationship. Before we react to our own thoughts and feelings or respond to the behaviours of others we have to have some understanding of what is going on in the mind behind them. We need to be able to mentalize. So it is a topic worth thinking about for all of us.

This book, in which the authors creatively piece together different aspects of mentalizing, explaining the process in an approachable way that does not require prior knowledge of formal psychology, is, in effect, a pathway to and a stimulus for mentalizing. Readers have to think about themselves and consider their own mentalizing and even how to apply it in their own personal, social, and work context. To this end there are a number of aspects to mentalizing that are useful to have some knowledge of—how does the brain learn to mentalize minds, what does it look like when it is being done well, how do we know when we and others are doing it badly, can we improve our mentalizing? Reflections on and answers to these questions can be found in this book.

There is no agreement about how humans develop the ability to mentalize as accurately as they do and there is debate within schools of philosophy of mind, psychology, and neuroscience subsumed under the rubric of social cognition, about how social and cultural processes become embedded in an individual and society. Understanding the foundations of social cognition is of considerable importance not only for the mental health of a population but also for effective and efficient functioning of social institutions such as schools, prisons, hospitals, care homes, and teams working together. Creating a mentalizing environment is likely to engender productive collaboration and learning. We feel cared about and considered as a person when we are mentalized, that someone sees things from our perspective and is respectful of our mental experience. This facilitates a level of trust in others and a sense that they have our best interests at heart. A school with mentalizing teachers sensitive to their pupil's minds would be predicted to have fewer behavioural problems and better learning outcomes than a school populated with low mentalizing teachers operating on, say, coercive and punitive behavioural systems. Indeed, this is the case. So it behoves us all to try to become better mentalizers of ourselves and others if we can. This book helps us begin to do that.

There are a number of ideas of how we learn to mentalize. Some argue that we have theories that we hold about how other minds work and we interact with others using those theories. Others suggest that this is not possible as we would have to have too many theories and it would be rather slow and not work seamlessly enough for social interaction. So it is argued that we manage to mentalize well by learning to put ourselves in others' shoes to model in our own minds what is happening in their mind. We simulate their experience and then respond according to that understanding. But more recently it has been argued that mentalizing is firmly embedded in childhood developmental processes and builds over time through interactional processes and there is no need to hold theories or to simulate experience. We learn from birth through attachment interaction and later affiliative relationships about how minds work and this process is embodied within us with perceptions linked to actions and responses. Sensory-motor processes of perception and action and emotional aspects of relationships are central to early developmental attachment processes, which allow the child to experience basic perceptions from interactionally based embodied learning of the intentions and emotions of themselves and then others. This is not mentally representational early in life but rather a primary subjectivity through which infants gain a perception-based understanding of other people's intentions and begin to respond reciprocally to them in line with their caregivers emotions. These dynamic processes transfer over time, becoming increasingly complex and refined through later relationships. So we embody within us an understanding of expressed intentions of others and how these are generally expressed through small gestures and bodily movements, facial expressions, vocalizations, and so on. Over time we engage with others in increasingly complex social exchanges and this allows us to hone our skills, particularly of embedding our primary subjective experiences of ourselves in what are called secondary intersubjective processes when we are required to move towards joint intention with others and to share mental states. In sum, it seems likely that no one theory of the development of efficient mentalizing processes transcends another and it is likely that we use all three mechanisms.

The authors of this book illustrate many aspects of effective mentalizing and ineffective mentalizing, so that the reader can begin to understand how to apply it to themselves and their own social interactions and consider being part of a mentalizing milieu. Taking the three developmental aspects underpinning mentalizing outlined earlier, we can suggest some top tips for mentalizing which are discussed further in this book—brainstorm theories about why someone is like they are—what is the most plausible explanation (theory); consciously put yourself in someone else's shoes and consider how you would experience something (simulation); share with someone else how you experience something while simultaneously trying to see things from their perspective (interactional). See how things go for you when you do these things. Good mentalizing tends to feed itself. Are the interactions more comfortable? Are the outcomes better?

Of course, mentalizing can go wrong for all of us and problems can become embedded over time. We all wrestle with it quite a lot of the time and as with most complex skills, it is easy to do badly, often regardless of how hard we try. Some feelings are complex and hard to pin down and intense emotions often disrupt mentalizing even though understanding feelings is one of the *lack of mentalization → mentalization becomes / replaced by assumptions*

primary tasks of mentalizing. Mentalizing of others is made even more difficult by the fact that people often do not want to reveal their mental state, and
so the evidence that we have about what they are really thinking may be much
less than we need. In this situation we make assumptions—sometimes wild
ones—about what people are thinking. This unbounded imagination can become the way our mind works most of the time and this is the case if the early
phases of development are persistently disrupted by stress for example due to
attachment trauma. The reciprocity of the attachment dynamic in trauma is
disorganized; learning about oneself becomes problematic and the responses
of others towards us is impossible to predict. The embedding of interactional
process fragments and serves only to create mental confusion. This engenders
fear of connection with others and a tendency for social isolation and with-
drawal from social communication and social learning. Mentalizing is shut
down and we begin to avoid our own states of mind as they are too painful and
those of others because how they see us is inconceivable. The social vigilance
that ensues is termed epistemic hypervigilance and precludes the individual
from joining in contexts where learning could take place. They are forced to
hide and, understandably, a wall of mistrust is set up. It is a long journey to
regain trust in the world which has only delivered pain. But understanding
how mentalizing works and beginning to open up one's mind to others is the
first step.

The quintessential aspect of this book is that it translates complex psychological understanding of human interaction into a comprehensible everyday
narrative. Readers will be able to relate to the only too human examples of
effective and ineffective mentalizing, and thereby use them to reflect on their
own mentalizing and how they function in everyday relationships. It is from
reflection that change becomes possible. So sit back, relax, read, and open up
your mind to mentalizing.

Anthony Bateman
London, 2023

Contents

1

Why this book?

Perhaps you find yourself getting into the same arguments with your partner over and over again. They seem to be about trivial things and yet you have often wondered why you just can't stop these arguments. Maybe you wonder why you have a lot of patience with your daughter, but not with your son. It is not that you love him any less. And yet you react differently to your two children. Perhaps you have felt helpless as a teacher. The approach that works with other children doesn't seem to work with that one pupil. Or maybe you can get along with most of your colleagues, but less with that one colleague that seems to trigger you over and over again.

And you? You suppress your irritation. Maybe you feel ashamed of some of your thoughts or feelings. Or you are disappointed that some things turn out differently than you would have liked. And yet: every human knows these struggles. Interactions with others do not always go the way we would like. We are not always the best version of ourselves. We sometimes overreact or make the same mistakes over and over again. We may feel misunderstood by others. Or conversely, we feel unable to reach someone else. These things can lead to misconceptions, misunderstandings, frustration, friction, and sometimes loneliness.

A major reason why things go wrong is because we cannot directly see the thoughts and feelings of others. We can think about them and we can try to imagine what they are like, but in doing so, we can be completely off the mark. And sometimes we just don't think about our own thoughts and feelings. We just act. Why? Just because!

Remember the last quarrel you had. What was it about? Probably the content wasn't even that important and yet the conversation derailed. Do you remember how you felt about that fight? And how do you think the other person felt? Or maybe you didn't argue explicitly, but the distance arose rather unspoken. Do you sometimes feel alone and misunderstood?

The Power of Mentalizing. Joost Hutsebaut, Liesbet Nijssens, and Miriam van Vessem, Oxford University Press.
© Joost Hutsebaut, Liesbet Nijssens, Miriam van Vessem 2023. DOI: 10.1093/oso/9780198880677.003.0001

Mentalizing and epistemic trust

This book is about humans, about relationships and interactions between them and about how these can go wrong sometimes. The basic idea could be summarized as follows: if we pay more attention to our own feelings, desires, and intentions and to those of others (i.e., *mentalizing* better), our contacts and relationships will become more pleasant, feel safer, and work better. In addition, we will be able to reach and help each other better (i.e., greater *epistemic trust*). This applies to relationships with parents, partners, and children, but also to our interactions with friends, clients, and colleagues.

Mentalizing is a complicated concept for an important and very natural process that we all know. It means that we try to understand our own behaviour and that of others from what could possibly lie behind that behaviour: someone's need, his or her intention, the feelings or expectations from which you or the other person act. Mentalizing implies not only looking at what the other is *doing*, but also trying to understand the *background* of this behaviour. We all do this, every day. If we see that our partner is sad, we wonder what's going on. We think about what could be wrong, whether we may have done something to upset our partner. Sometimes you find yourself reacting very strongly to someone and you wonder where that sudden reaction comes from. You wonder why you got frustrated so quickly: Is yesterday's argument still bothering you? Or did you have a difficult day at work? Or ... there are so many reasons why you may have lashed out at the other person.

Mentalizing enables epistemic trust. Epistemic trust refers to the ability to trust others and learn from them. It refers to believing that others can offer and teach you something valuable. In clinical practice, we sometimes talk about people 'feeling mentalized': they experience feeling understood and recognized in their inner world. From that experience, they open up to the perspective of the other person. When you feel that someone else really understands your terrible situation from within, you will find it easier to take him or her more seriously. Mentalizing therefore enables you to reach someone.

This may sound simple and self-evident. Yet, there is a lot of theory and research behind this basic theorem. Often complicated theories about how we grow up as people and how this turns us into the person we are today, about how we form and shape relationships (*attachment* and attachment styles) and about the knowledge we acquire in interaction with others (*epistemic trust*). With this book we want to make these rich theories accessible, and moreover applicable in daily life: within your relationship, your family, your group of friends, and at work. Because we believe that more focused attention to mentalizing and epistemic trust can help us be the better version of ourselves a little more often.

> Take some time to consider what you expect from this book. What do you hope to learn? What do you need? Do you often contemplate about yourself and others? Do you find it easy to deal with your emotions? Or do you find this sentimental and soft? Are you more the kind of person who just goes ahead and does things?

concrete behavioural advice can fail because a behaviour can be overdetermined

Before you read any further, we want to give you a warning. This is not a classic self-help book in which you will find concrete behavioural advice that will allow you to always react in the right way. This book contains many tips, but no quick-fix solutions. Our 'advices' are not so concrete or directly applicable that you immediately know what to say or do in various difficult relational situations. We cannot tell you how you can change your irritation towards your colleague or how you can have more patience with your son. If there was this kind of advice that would always work, parenting would be child's play, and any relationship would run smoothly. However, we do think that we can describe the pathway how to better understand these situations and thus be able to deal with them better. It is not without reason that the given advices are not very concrete. We think that such behavioural advice is doomed to fail because it ignores the underlying meaning of behaviour. The same behaviour can have different grounds. Suppose someone wants to advice you on what to do so you will be less likely to lash out at your partner. The content of that advice may depend on why you lashed out at your partner. If this happened once—for example, because an argument from the day before was still bothering you—then the best advice may be to talk to your partner about that incident and clear the air. But if you flew off the handle because you have been feeling overworked at your job for months and are therefore much more irritable at home, the appropriate advice is clearly different. The point is: The best advice can only be given if you know the specific meaning of the behaviour in this specific situation. Moreover, the advice will usually only be internalized in an inter-*advice can only penetrate if the interaction is sincere (experience of living heard)*-action in which real contact is experienced. Therefore, the tips and tricks in this book refer to the mentalizing process that is necessary to better understand behaviour and to reinstate a true connection to others. This process will then allow you to decide for yourself how to act differently or better in the relevant situation.

Behaviour and what lies behind it

Humans are social beings. How we think or feel about ourselves is often determined by how we experience our interactions with others. You feel valuable as a parent if you feel that you have a good connection with your child. As a partner, you feel appreciated when you notice that the other person cares about you. When something is not going well, we are often tempted to try to change the other person's behaviour. The behaviour is the most visible and tangible port of entry to change something within the relationship. A man asks his wife to be more considerate so that he is able to feel that she cares. A mother wants her child to act polite when visiting others so that she can be proud. How many parenting books exist that teach us how to control a child's behaviour? How often have you prescribed 'behaviour' to your partner?

However, behaviour is only the physical expression of a variety of possible intentional experiences and internal mental states. This makes it hard to influence behaviour without paying attention to the underlying thoughts, feelings, and desires. Even more fundamental is that by only focusing on behaviour, we miss something essential that is much more important than the behaviour that is expressed. Let's clarify this point with two examples.

Christopher and Olivia
Christopher is a primary school teacher. A girl in his class, Olivia, regularly disrupts the lessons. She can get very angry and frequently gets into fights with her classmates. Her classmates are afraid of her and no one likes to sit next to her in class.

> Take a moment to reflect on this example. What are your thoughts and feelings? How would you react when Olivia reacts hostile and angry for the umpteenth time? Why would you react in that way?

Olivia's behaviour is difficult to handle in class, she disrupts the lessons and other children are afraid of her. Other parents have complained about their kids being hit or kicked by Olivia. Olivia's behaviour must be stopped.

Christopher decided to implement a reward system for the group. After two months of working with this system, it seems to pay off. The group is calmer and Olivia is also doing better in class. Olivia's disturbing behaviour has not completely stopped, but it gradually decreases. Olivia has learned to control her behaviour better. Off course, this is a fine approach that usually works for Olivia and Christopher as well as for her classmates. But still there are instances when Olivia is no longer able to control her behaviour and gets disruptive again. Actually, she remains a bit of a problem child, and the other children keep their distance. Olivia also feels that they continue to approach her somewhat differently, but she does not really understand why: she does control herself most of the time, doesn't she?

Although the behavioural approach has brought some peace and Olivia's behaviour did also actually change, still something essential has remained unchanged in how Olivia feels and sees herself. Similarly, despite her improved behaviour, nothing essentially seems to have changed in how others perceive Olivia. Olivia continues to see herself as a 'problem child' that no one really likes. Others continue to approach her as 'difficult' and unpredictable. The behaviour is under control, but the underlying representations remain the same. Hence, no matter how important this approach may be in education or in working with a class, it is still lacking something: something that can fundamentally change Olivia and her relationships with others.

> Before you continue reading, take a minute to think about what it's like for Olivia to be in this class. How would she feel? How do others perceive her? How does she experience the image others have of her?

Christopher's classroom is quieter and more peaceful, but he notices that Olivia is still not feeling well. He thinks that in group assignments she often does not quite belong. The other students react slightly differently to her. During a group assignment, Olivia becomes irritated after Grace from her group does not respond to her input. Olivia starts to speak louder, but it seems that this only results in group members taking her even less seriously. Suddenly, Olivia pushes the table away and shouts that the other group members are losers. While observing this from a distance, Christopher notices that he is not only annoyed by the way things are getting out of hand, but he also feels something of Olivia's sadness. He considers that Olivia seems to become rebellious and annoying when she feels ignored. Possibly, she has little confidence that she belongs to the group. When the other group members act more prudent and distant towards her, these feelings seem only to be confirmed to her. By reflecting on Olivia this way, Christopher is starting to feel more empathy for the underlying intentions and feelings of Olivia that cause her reactions. He decides to talk to her after class:

> *'You might expect me to be mad at you because things didn't go well in class, but I'd like to talk to you about what happened within you and why it went wrong this way. I think I also saw how you really did your best to fit in and to participate. Am I correct?'*

What would be the impact on Olivia? Probably she is a bit surprised because the expected punishment did not follow. Perhaps she feels very seen and understood because Christopher is able to look beyond her behaviour.

> *Christopher: 'It feels to me that it was especially unpleasant for you when Grace did not respond to your proposal.' 'Yes, she acts as if I am not allowed to participate with the others,' Olivia adds, gazing at her feet. Christopher nods. 'I don't know if this is what Grace intended, but I did notice that her comment hurt you.' 'Yes, they just shut me out!' Christopher mirrors: 'That sounds very sad, as if you really wanted to do your best and it was very painful for you because the others didn't seem to notice.' Olivia looks up: 'Yes, then I feel so stupid that I can only react with anger.'*

Christopher goes beyond setting limits to Olivia's behaviour. Of course, she shouldn't misbehave like that in class. However, he pauses to consider what causes her behaviour and he helps her to think about that as well. This way, he helps her to better understand her own behaviour and to better understand the impact on the other children in the group and how they subsequently react to her.

What happens in this example is that Christopher started *mentalizing* about Olivia. This creates something of an understanding within himself and between them. He makes it safe for Olivia to reflect on herself. He creates a bond with Olivia and helps her better understand and regulate herself and her relationships with others. Of course, this is not achieved by having a one-time conversation, but by constantly encouraging her to pay attention to what she experiences within herself and how this may affect her own behaviour. But also, to pay attention to what's happening in the interaction with her classmates and how this may affect what she and others are experiencing.

The reward system teaches Olivia to control her behaviour. That is important and pleasant: for Olivia—because she is now less often seen as 'disturbing' or 'difficult'—and for Christopher and the rest of the class—because she no longer disrupts lessons and no longer approaches other children aggressively. By also approaching her in a mentalizing way, Olivia feels understood in her fears and sadness about the way things are going in the classroom. Olivia doesn't just learn to control her behaviour. She also learns to better understand her behaviour and thus her emotions, and therefore to regulate them better. A mentalizing approach influences the quality of the relationship between Christopher and Olivia. It also impacts the self-image of Olivia, who had become convinced that she *is* a difficult child. Probably, this may soon also affect the image that others in the class have of Olivia. In addition to controlling her behaviour, Olivia learns many important things that can help her in the rest of her life: instead of being a difficult child, she is a person with emotions and behaviours, which she can learn to understand and therefore learn to manage better. This latter is precisely the most valuable lesson she learns and can capture for the rest of her life.

Let's look at a second example that can further clarify what we mean.

Jonathan and Kathleen
Jonathan and Kathleen have been together for twelve years. Last year they went through a tough relationship crisis. Jonathan has had an affair with a colleague at work. Jonathan and Kathleen broke up briefly but got back together. Jonathan has changed jobs. He has been extra attentive since the incident. He makes sure he is home on time, buys flowers and tells Kathleen more often than before that he loves her. Still, Kathleen's distrust remains. They also never really talk about what happened anymore. Jonathan finds it frustrating that Kathleen cannot get past the incident. Isn't he doing everything to make it clear to her that he was wrong? When will it be enough for her? Kathleen, on her part, notices that she no longer trusts him. Who says it won't happen again?

Jonathan and Kathleen are at an impasse. Since the incident, Jonathan's behaviour has been impeccable. Yet, this does not change the image Kathleen has of him, nor the trust she places in him. This is frustrating for Jonathan: he behaves reliably, but he *is* not reliable in the eyes of Kathleen. Just like with Olivia, something essential is lacking to really bring about change. It could be that Jonathan's trustworthy behaviour does not register with Kathleen. More than that, it may only make her more suspicious: why is he showing off so much? Is there more to hide? How can she ever trust him again? This is also frustrating for Kathleen: she wants to be able to trust him again, but she can't.

We do not know whether their relationship will recover from this incident. Nevertheless, the above example is perhaps relatable to many of us. We can also think about what Kathleen might need to become less suspicious so that her damaged trust can really start to heal. Could it be that Kathleen has to feel that Jonathan fully understands how painful and hurtful the incident has been for her in order to re-establish the connection between them?

We all mentalize, but there is a world to win by paying more attention to it. Being seen and feeling understood is an important necessity of life and partly determines how you feel about yourself and the world. This book brings together what we know about healthy development, attachment, security, resilience, trust, learning from others, and mentalizing, and is illustrated with recognizable examples. Based on knowledge from attachment and developmental theories, it provides insight into how to improve any relationship, whether it is professional or private. We hope this book is not only very rich in knowledge, but above all that it will help the reader to occasionally become a better version of him- or herself.

2

What is mentalizing?

As humans, we need relationships. However, it is annoying that those relationships do not always run smoothly. Often, our conflicts and irritations have their roots in misunderstandings. Why doesn't he clean up his mess when I ask him every morning? Why is she so defensive when I try to help her? Mentalizing can be the key to mutual understanding, and subsequently remove an important breeding ground for conflict. In this chapter, we explore the process of mentalizing based on a case example that plays in secondary education: math teacher Eric tries to get a grip on the troublesome behaviour of fifteen-year-old Nathan.

Eric and Nathan

Eric is a teacher. Last year, he has had a difficult time at school. As a mentor, he was responsible for a class that caused a lot of problems. His gentle approach didn't actually work well. In addition, he had also been sick for a while and it had taken time to recover, which prevented him from putting the energy into his class that might have been needed. It was even more annoying that he had felt a bit judged in the teachers' room. His colleagues didn't say it in that many words, but for Eric it felt as if his colleagues thought he should have taken a tougher stance in the class last year. This school year, he is therefore keen to avoid such hassle. He has heard from a colleague that he should especially be paying attention to Nathan. Since last year, he has started to cause more and more problems—especially in mathematics, the subject that Eric teaches.

Fifteen-year-old Nathan is a good student, but he doesn't like math at all. He also had no connection with his math teacher last year, who could make comments that made him feel even more insecure and stupid. He is not very sure of himself and was bullied by some of the boys in his class last school year. Therefore, he finds the start of the school year quite stressful. Fortunately, he is rid of his old math teacher. He has heard about his successor that he cannot keep order.

Immediately, in the first weeks of school, it becomes apparent to Eric what his colleague meant: Nathan is often doing other things during math class.

The Power of Mentalizing. Joost Hutsebaut, Liesbet Nijssens, and Miriam van Vessem, Oxford University Press.
© Joost Hutsebaut, Liesbet Nijssens, Miriam van Vessem 2023. DOI: 10.1093/oso/9780198880677.003.0002

Talking to classmates, drawing in his exercise book—the math material seems to be of little interest to him. He often does not do his homework or does it half-heartedly. Even worse: when Eric asks him questions, he responds with jokes, which causes hilarity in class. Eric intends to keep Nathan on a short leash. At all costs, he wants to prevent things from getting out of hand again this year. How would he be able to explain that to his colleagues?

In turn, Nathan was already worried that he would not feel a 'connection' with his new math teacher. And yes, right in the first weeks, Eric addresses him more strictly and distantly than his classmates. Like his predecessor, Eric seems to want to make a mockery of him in front of the class. Why do they always have to pick on him? He already has such problems with math. He tries to stay cool about it. He especially does not want the other students to notice that it hurts him, because then—of course—the bullying will start all over again.

One day, when Nathan hasn't done his homework again, Eric resolutely sends him out of class. He wants to make a point. Nathan has been warned before and now he just has to experience the consequences. However, things go differently than Eric had expected. Nathan refuses to leave the classroom and says that others are not sent away for not doing their homework. He blames Eric for picking on him and makes it clear to him that he won't be treated like a wimp. For Eric, that's the final straw ... He sends Nathan home and informs him that he will call his parents to let them know about his behaviour in class. Nathan is not allowed to return to his lessons until he agrees to do what he is asked to do and he can show respect for his teacher.

However, after Eric has sanctioned Nathan, Eric feels unhappy about it. He is wondering whether he has gone too far. He feels unsure of himself and stays in his classroom after class so he doesn't have to talk to his colleagues for a while. Nathan is of course upset with Eric, but he is also angry with himself. Why did he let himself go like that? Why couldn't Eric act normally? He is afraid of how his parents will react: they already feel that he is not doing his best.

Eric observes Nathan's behaviour; he assesses it and responds to it. What Eric sees on the outside is Nathan's physical, visible behaviour: making jokes during class, sitting with his back turned and constantly talking to class-mates, and doing none or half of the homework assignments. This behaviour is interpreted by Eric: he interprets it as a sign that Nathan does not take the lessons seriously, is not interested in mathematics, is mainly concerned with impressing his friends, and perhaps, does not take him—Eric—seriously. That interpretation is perhaps coloured somewhat by the fact that he had already been warned about Nathan by a colleague. But what is especially significant, is his fear of a repetition of the disciplinary problem that he has already been confronted with the year before and the opinion of his colleagues that he felt about it. He wants to prove himself. It is therefore clear to him that Nathan's behaviour must stop. Eric does what many teachers might do: keep a close eye on Nathan, hold him accountable for his behaviour, threaten with sanctions, and ultimately sanction effectively. Perhaps the last sanction also followed because Eric does not know what to do anymore. In any case, Nathan will not embarrass him again in front of his colleagues!

Give meaning to behaviour

People have an inside and an outside. We can only perceive that outside directly. We cannot see the inside, however. We must interpret this from the visible part. This is not always easy. After all, the same behaviour can express different things. The process by which we nevertheless give meaning to our own behaviour and that of others is called *mentalizing*. This is an ongoing process. Sometimes conscious and thoughtful, but usually automatic and spontaneous.

Eric also gives meaning to Nathan's behaviour. He does this quickly and almost automatically. It is likely that Eric hasn't thought long about the meaning of Nathan's behaviour. Conversely, Nathan does not seem to think any deeper about Eric's behaviour. If we take a closer look at the interpretations of Eric and Nathan, two things stand out. First, the *content*: Eric and Nathan colour their interpretation in a certain, *personal* way: Eric thinks that Nathan wants to affect him in some way, and wants to embarrass him. Nathan, on the other hand, thinks that Eric picks on him. Second, the *shape*: Eric and Nathan both *know* for sure. They don't really consider other possible reasons why the other person is behaving this way. It 'feels' like this, so it 'is' like this.

The way in which we give meaning to our own reactions and those of others often gives direction to the behaviour that we subsequently display. You can also notice this in our example. Even those who are not a teacher can imagine something about Eric's reaction. Nathan's irritating behaviour almost forces sanctions. Behaviour sometimes has negative effects, and as a teacher or parent we set limits to contain those negative effects. However, Eric goes one step further, which may have to do with how he gives meaning to Nathan's behaviour. Eric 'knows' that Nathan is challenging his authority and 'therefore' he must be strict. Eric feels embarrassed by Nathan and not taken seriously, and he labels Nathan's problem as a problem of authority. He pushes the problem towards Nathan, as it were. That reaction is perhaps reinforced by Eric's fear that if he does not set limits for Nathan, half the class will soon question his authority. And Nathan? Well, we can imagine that Nathan senses some of the tension in Eric. He interprets it as: Eric doesn't like me. In fact, he picks on me. And this may also colour his reaction: in turn, he reacts firmly, and does not let himself be intimidated. He pushes the problem back: he doesn't feel a connection with Eric. And so, there may have been something going on between Eric and Nathan for a while that eventually gets out of hand in that particular lesson. Both will stand their ground in response to each other. The interaction hardens and both become stubborn. And they may both touch something vulnerable in the other. Perhaps Nathan feels more of a problem child and becomes more insecure about himself. And vice versa, Eric may also feel more insecure as a teacher.

Do Eric and Nathan interpret each other's behaviour correctly? Maybe not quite. The fact that Nathan is uninterested, doesn't want to do his best and wants to compromise Eric's authority is one possible explanation. However, because this example allows us to look inside Nathan's head, we also know that he feels insecure about mathematics and that he was bullied last year and doesn't want to end up in that position again. Nathan's jokes and apparent indifference may not mean so much that he wants to attack Eric personally, as that he wants to hide his insecurity so that he doesn't end up in a bad position again. Likewise, Eric's behaviour is perhaps more prompted by his fear of losing control of his class and thereby losing face towards his colleagues, than by a personal aversion to Nathan. Even one step further, we notice that in their interaction with each other, both show exactly the behaviour that strengthens the other in his assumptions: Eric becomes stricter and more distant, which perhaps confirms Nathan's assumption that Eric does not like him; and Nathan becomes more untouchable, perhaps reinforcing Eric's fear that Nathan will undermine his authority.

We're not quite done with the example yet. After all, Eric and Nathan do not live in a world of their own. Eric is part of a team of teachers and Nathan is a pupil. In this example, it matters. Apparently, the teachers' team did not really talk about the disciplinary problems that Eric had to deal with. Nevertheless, Eric felt judged by his colleagues. He was warned about Nathan, but did that help him in his interactions with him? And Nathan feels unsafe in the group, and that also influences his reaction. He didn't connect with the previous math teacher and he has heard stories about Eric. In this example, neither Eric nor Nathan is helped by their environment to make the interaction between them run smoothly. More specifically, the environment does not help them to cope with their own stress at the start of the school year and to stay in tune with each other in a good way and to assign a correct meaning to the other's behaviour.

This example shows how quickly an interaction between people can go wrong. In the classroom, at home or at work. Things went wrong between Eric and Nathan because they may not have been able to regulate their own stress sufficiently at the start of the new school year and partly because of this—in combination with not being helped by their environment—they make multiple assumptions about each other. Things go wrong because they don't mentalize well about themselves and others.

Implicit and explicit mentalizing

The meaning we give to our own behaviour and that of others is what we call *mentalizing*. Mentalizing refers to the process in which we give meaning to our own behaviour as well as to the behaviour of others, based on what we think is behind that behaviour—the reason why someone behaves this way or that way. Think of the intention that someone has, the expectations of the other, and a certain feeling from which you react. Feelings, intentions, and expectations are mental states—they take place in our head.

> **Mentalizing** = Understanding one's own behaviour and the behaviour of others from the perspective of underlying feelings, thoughts, intentions, and desires (*mental states*).

Mentalizing is the foundation of social relationships: without this unique quality, relationships between people are doomed to fail. It is conceivable that throughout evolution, people who were better at mentalizing were better equipped to survive. If you miss that quality, the behaviour of others simply cannot be understood. Others then become unpredictable and scary.

Mentalizing means recognizing that what we and others do is not meaningless. Behaviour expresses something, and has a purpose or *intention*. And behaviour has an *effect*. It affects ourselves and others. From there, interactions arise. I want or feel something and do something; what I do has an effect upon the other, who experiences and feels something about it, and reacts from that experience; this reaction then has an impact on me, so that I feel or experience something again. The better we slow down mentally and reflect on our own needs, feelings and wishes, and the better we think about the effects of what we do on others (on their feelings, expectations, needs, etc.), the more predictable and understandable the response of the other may become. In an interaction in which both parties mentalize well, there is alignment and mutual understanding so that the interaction runs more smoothly. Conversely, interactions resulting from poor mentalizing will be less smooth and constructive.

Mentalizing is usually automatic and implicit. We really don't spend all day consciously thinking about what we feel and think, why we do what we do or what others might communicate when they do something. Most interactions between people follow a certain set of patterns, which do not necessarily make it a necessity to think explicitly about the feelings and intentions involved in these interactions. If you come home after a working day, you may have several regular interactions with your partner. Maybe you give him or her a hug, ask how the day was, and discuss who will do the cooking and who will help the children with their homework. You listen to your partner's experiences, tell something about yourself, and ask the children how their school day was. You are attuned to your partner and children, but that may be largely implicit or automatic. As long as the actual interaction roughly follows the set pattern, there is no reason to change that automatic, implicit process.

But suppose that one day your partner is sitting on the couch crying when you get home. Then you may focus your attention more on his or her mental state: what's going on? Why are you crying? You consciously slow down and think about what is going on, about how your partner feels and about what touched him or her. If you succeed, your contact usually improves: the other feels understood, and the interaction deepens. But suppose you come home, and your partner reacts in an irritated way, for example, by making a critical remark. Then it often takes a very conscious effort to tune in to the reasons behind the irritated comment. Perhaps it is easier to respond with irritation. This can lead to increasing tension and an unpleasant interaction. In that interaction, there is a good chance that both partners no longer mentalize well about each other. For example, that they become reproachful: 'You must always criticize!' 'You never do what I ask you to do!'

A vulnerable capacity

Mentalizing is one of the most uniquely human traits, but at the same time there is great variation in its quality and effectiveness, both between and within individuals. On a daily basis, we all recognize moments in ourselves when we mentalize well (effectively), but also: less well (ineffectively). For example, we no longer think about what is happening, here and now, to ourselves and the other, and we revert to *automatic assumptions*. It is often about things that we find typical of the other, about patterns that we think we recognize in them. In other words, we fall into *stereotypical* thinking. Eric and Nathan also seem to have reached a point where they lose themselves in general 'truths' about each other: Eric thinks that Nathan has a problem with authority and is *always* deliberately embarrassing him; Nathan thinks that Eric picks on him and wants to embarrass him. When we fall into ineffective mentalizing—for example, under stress or heightened arousal—we are no longer properly attuned to the other person's *actual* intentions. Instead, we rely upon quick and automatic assumptions and often tend to do things in a way that is rather coloured by our own vulnerabilities. In other words, our beliefs at such a moment often say something about ourselves.

> Consider a recent, nasty experience in connecting with someone important to you. For example, an argument or an uncomfortable moment. Do you remember what beliefs about yourself and the other came to your mind at the time? When you blame someone, what is the first thing that comes to your mind? If someone touches you or makes you insecure, what is it that affects you the most?

We all regress into ineffective mentalizing from time to time. We may interpret behaviour too quickly, without even being aware of the fact that it is 'only' an interpretation. We then assume that what we see and think is 'true'. What we think and feel about ourselves and others is the only correct explanation. Eric 'knows' that Nathan is challenging him. He no longer pays attention to the fact that this is his interpretation of Nathan's intention. What I think, is real. I feel annoyed, so he is annoying. Moreover, if Eric 'knows' that Nathan is embarrassing him, then it is very logical that this causes tension or irritation. At such a moment, Eric experiences Nathan as a student who *deliberately* embarrasses him. He won't let that happen! It may not be surprising that this often leads to escalation and mutual misunderstanding. Moreover, poor mentalizing is often contagious: if Eric no longer thinks about Nathan and reacts from irritation, then there is a good chance that Nathan will no longer be able to think about Eric's reaction and will therefore join the game of overbidding. 'Hear him mouthing again' will set in motion a different pattern of communication than 'He acts so tough when he feels very insecure'. The fact that both, at some point, no longer mentalize well does not mean that Eric is a bad teacher or that Nathan is an annoying teenager. Rather, it shows that the ability to mentalize effectively is fragile and that we can lose it quickly.

Dimensions of mentalizing

Mentalizing is a process that constantly takes place in our head. Usually, it takes place *implicitly* and we are not so aware of it. Sometimes we switch to *explicit* mentalizing. Consider the example of the partner who reacts differently than we expect. We then think much more consciously about behaviour and give it meaning more consciously. Mentalizing explicitly means 'slowing down': you slow down your thought process to really dwell on what you feel and think or what the other person might feel and think. Hence, implicit and explicit mentalizing are two dimensions of the mentalizing process.

In addition, we can distinguish between mentalizing about *ourselves* and about *others*. You can reflect on your own feelings, thoughts, needs, expectations, and disappointments to better understand your own behaviour or your tendency to do something. Or you can consider what the other person would think, feel, want, and expect in order to understand why he or she reacts that way. In line with this, we can mentalize from within ourselves or others. This is more about the form, *how* we mentalize (rather than the content or object of mentalizing). For example, the way in which you look at yourself, but also at others, can be completely determined by your own perspective (self), whereby you do not allow yourself to be 'informed' by signals from others. For example, 'I know what the other is thinking or feeling', without really empathizing with the other's perspective. Or: the image I have of myself is purely based on my own feelings and thoughts and does not consider how others experience me. Conversely, there may be too little individuality or there may be a tendency to merge with others. How you look at yourself and others is interpreted from a focus on others (other). For example, I do everything I can to please the other person and am hypersensitive to signs of rejection that determine how I view myself, namely a worthless person. Such polarizations on the self-other dimension are manifestations of ineffective mentalizing. Effective mentalizing takes information from yourself and others into account to form an image of yourself and others.

Further, mentalizing can be *internally* or *externally* oriented. When mentalizing is externally oriented, you particularly pay attention to external cues (from yourself or others). You hear that the other person has a certain intonation, or you see a frown and that makes you think he is angry or irritated. The external signal 'intonation' or 'frown' evokes a certain meaning. Regarding yourself, the focus can also be on external signals (e.g., bags under the eyes, stomach pain, clothing): 'my shoulders are completely cramped by the tensions'. When mentalizing is internally focused, you focus more on what is going on in your own inner world or that of others. If your girlfriend has not been hired for a job, you can imagine that it must be very painful for her because she is already very insecure about herself.

Finally, mentalizing may be more related to feelings (*affects*) or more to thoughts (*cognitions*). Formally, mentalizing can result from 'sympathizing' (as with empathy) or 'feeling through' (affective). Rationalization, seeking explanations, or reasoning are examples of the cognitive pole. For example, you can ask yourself what someone thinks or means (cognitive/other) or what is the reason why you want to get out of a situation (cognitive/self), you may be touched (affective/self) or ask yourself why something affects you so (cognitive/self), or you can empathize with your child (affective/other).

Dimensions of mentalizing
- Automatic/implicit—controlled/explicit
- Self—other
- Internal—external
- Cognitive—affective

Consider how mentalizing works for you. Are you often explicitly concerned with how you feel or how others feel, or does it happen more automatically and implicitly? In the first case, does that sometimes result in worrying excessively or, in the second case, in making assumptions too fast? Do you rather think about yourself, or are you very focused on what others might think and feel? Are you sensitive to external signals, such as someone's posture, gaze, intonation, or facial expression? Are you sometimes too sensitive to it? Do you pay attention to your own inner world (what you yourself experience, think, or feel) or do you sometimes ignore it? Are you more analytical and rational (thoughts) or more affective and intuitive (feelings)?

A mentalizing stance

In this section, we will consider one of the most important characteristics of effective mentalizing: the *mentalizing stance*. This means that you do not limit yourself to what someone is doing or how someone is acting, but try to understand from which feelings, thoughts, needs, or expectations someone is acting. You are curious about these mental states, even though you know that you can never be sure of what is going on in the other person's mind, and you are open to it.

A mentalizing stance refers to being *humble* and recognizing that we can never be sure why someone is doing something, even if you are that 'someone' yourself. We are not talking about repressed unconscious processes here. What we mean is that mental processes are 'layered': you react irritated, but if you think about it a little longer, it may feel more like sadness. So even 'knowing' that you are irritated does not have to be as obvious or 'certain' as it may seem at first glance. Look at Eric: perhaps his overt irritation also covers some feelings of impotence and maybe even shame or fear. And he also has to slow himself down to make contact with that shame or fear: 'in the heat of the moment' he may just feel irritated.

Those who mentalize well nevertheless adopt a *curious* attitude or *inquisitive* stance: *I am not sure what is going on with the other person (or myself), but I do want to know.* You notice that your colleague reacts somewhat differently compared to her usual reaction, and you are curious about what could be going on. Think back to the example of Eric and Nathan: both thought they knew for sure why the other did what he did. They both lacked the curiosity and openness needed to really understand the other. Good mentalizing encompasses knowing that you cannot be sure of what the other person is thinking, feeling, or meaning. Mentalizing is tolerating uncertainty and realizing that your interpretation is one of many.

> Nothing more annoying than someone who 'knows' what you think and feel. Put it to the test and role-play with your partner or colleague: he or she tells you something that happened that day. If you think you understand what happened and what it was like for the other person, then you are certain: you know what everyone meant and felt. What is the effect on your partner or colleague?

Just because effective mentalizing involves realizing that you can never be sure of your assumptions about mental states (feelings, thoughts), it also means recognizing that you sometimes must adjust your interpretation: 'I thought you were angry with me, but now I understand that you were mainly concerned about me.' We must be open to what is going on in the other person's mind and—if necessary—be flexible enough to adjust our hypotheses about it.

A mentalizing stance is characterized by:
- Modesty: you never know for sure;
- Curiosity: I am not sure what is going on with the other (or myself), but I do want to know;
- Openness and flexibility: I could be wrong and may need to adjust my interpretation.

Hence, good mentalizing implies paying attention to all aspects of your own mental world and that of others, that is, both cognitions and affects. Further, it implies that you pay attention to both external and internal signals. However, it does not mean that you constantly think consciously about the reasons behind the behaviour of yourself and others, but that you mentalize implicitly when possible and shift smoothly when explicit mentalizing is needed. Implicit mentalizing saves time and energy, but sometimes you have to consciously slow down and pause to understand something properly.

So, drawing conclusions about someone too quickly does not go hand in hand with a mentalizing stance. Sometimes, we tend to explain behaviour from labels. We could then say that Nathan behaves annoyingly because he has attention deficit hyperactivity disorder (ADHD) or because he is highly intelligent. Similarly, it could be argued that Nathan behaves annoyingly because he has a hard time at home or because he has a problem with authority. These are typical examples of poor mentalizing. After all, the question is whether such labels provide a sufficient explanation. ADHD, intelligence, a difficult home situation, and authority problems do not show up with that one teacher or in that one lesson, only to disappear the next hour. And yet, you often see that the student shows those 'problems with authority' in interaction with one teacher and not necessarily shows them with others. The value of such statements is therefore often quite limited. Moreover, they prevent us from thinking further. It may be reassuring for Eric to think that Nathan has authority problems. This explains Nathan's behaviour as a result of something in Nathan (and not in himself). Eric no longer has to ask himself what exactly happens in his lesson or between them. From a mentalizing perspective you want to understand why this child (with ADHD, high intelligence, and a problematic home situation) shows this behaviour exactly now (in this lesson, in this interaction): what is currently going on in the mind of this child that could explain the current behaviour?

At other times it is not very convenient to mentalize explicitly. If you read and understand the other too well in early love relationships, the infatuation may not start properly. It is more pleasant to maintain the illusion that you are in a bubble together, in which you feel the other person perfectly and are completely on the same page. Love is indeed blind. Even in dangerous situations, you should not think too much, but act. When you are threatened with a knife, you do not want to understand the motives of the perpetrator. Once the danger has passed, it is important to give explicit meaning to what happened to you.

Moreover, good mentalizing is not always easy to recognize. People sometimes seem to mentalize well, for example, because they are very focused on the intentions or feelings of others, but they lack the uncertainty that characterizes good mentalizing. For example, they go way too far in interpreting possible intentions, far beyond what one could reasonably assume. Or sometimes people ruminate about themselves and others. Consequently, they lose themselves in endless thinking about why others have done and said something. Mentalizing then loses its purpose and may rather become a way to gain control. Yet another variation is that people abuse their mentalizing skills. Here, they pick up on the vulnerability of the other, which could be the start of good mentalizing, but then misuse that knowledge, for example, to control the other.

Restore effective mentalizing

Effective mentalizing is frequently lost, but fortunately we can restore it. Let's go back to Eric and Nathan.

Eric feels uncomfortable that things got so out of hand with Nathan that day. At the end of the day, he sees Hannah, a colleague. She was very supportive last year when he was having such a hard time. Hannah asks him why he did not appear in the teachers' room that afternoon. Eric is happy to be able to talk to someone. He feels that he can open up to Hannah. He tells her how the incident with Nathan is bothering him. He wonders aloud whether he has overreacted because he was afraid that the classroom situation might get out of hand. 'What did Nathan do today that made you react so angry?' Hannah asks him. Eric thinks: 'It is so difficult for me to reach him. He doesn't react to my limit setting which makes me feel so helpless.' He tells Hannah that he was warned about Nathan and that this caused tension from the start. Eric then realizes that he was punitive towards Nathan from the beginning. He realizes that he doesn't really know why Nathan behaves like he does in class.

After the conversation with Hannah, Eric decides to call Nathan. On the phone, he mentions that he regrets that things got so out of hand and that he first wants to talk to Nathan about it before calling his parents or the headmaster. He suggests that Nathan comes in before classes start the next day. Nathan is surprised by Eric's phone call. He is very pleased that Eric immediately says that he is not happy with how he handled things. He was worried that he would be blamed, and he notices that Eric's phone call is reducing the tension. He also realizes that he has not always been the easiest person to deal with.

Eric met with Hannah, whom he trusts and with whom he feels safe. Listening to Hannah and the questions she asked helped Eric to restore mentalizing. In fact, the mentalizing recovery process was already underway: Immediately after class, Eric was less sure of his case and was doubting his reaction. He tried to understand his own strong reaction. The mentalizing stance of Hannah helped him. She first asked questions that allowed him to better place his own emotional response. As a result, he started mentalizing explicitly about himself: slowing down and dwelling on what exactly affected him. Then, he was also able to mentalize better about Nathan. He realized that he doesn't really have an idea why Nathan behaves that way in his lessons. Eric enabled himself to focus on the mental states of Nathan, beyond his behaviour. He switched from implicit to explicit mentalizing and became curious about the inner world of Nathan. Therefore, he was more open to interpretations that deviated from his original hypothesis.

Reinstating mentalizing immediately affected the contact with Nathan. Instead of pushing the problem back to Nathan, Eric turned it into a joint problem. He was open about his own experience ('I'm sorry …'). The recovered mentalizing of Eric was also 'contagious' and promoted mentalizing in Nathan. In turn, he will be more open to Eric in a conversation.

> Consider the following two scenarios: How would the conversation with Nathan and his parents have gone if Eric and Nathan had not restored their mentalizing? And how might the conversation unfold after their mentalizing has recovered?

Mentalizing creates space. Eric no longer feels the need to guard his authority because he 'knows' that Nathan is out to undermine it. Nathan no longer feels the need to adopt an untouchable attitude because he 'knows' that Eric is out to embarrass him. If both had not recovered their mentalizing stance, their defences would probably fall on deaf ears, but additionally, this interaction would repeat itself sooner rather than later. In fact, the actions that follow from ineffective mentalizing (Eric: more severe and punitive; Nathan: more indifferent and unattainable) could lead to a further exacerbation of this pattern. After all: it is precisely Eric's strict behaviour that prompts Nathan to adopt an indifferent attitude, and it is precisely Nathan's indifference that prompts Eric to become even stricter. But perhaps most importantly, such interactions will further reinforce the vulnerabilities in the image that Eric and Nathan have of themselves and of others. For example, Eric will feel more insecure as a teacher and, as a result, may also experience his students and colleagues as more threatening.

Summary

Mentalizing is the process by which we give meaning to our own behaviour and that of others from the mental states that lie behind it, such as feelings, needs, and expectations. It allows us to do what we physically cannot do: look inside our own head and the heads of others. As a result, we can better understand ourselves and others and behaviour also become more predictable. Without this capacity, human relationships would go horribly wrong. In this chapter, we have discussed the various features of this mentalizing process. Probably the most important characteristic of a mentalizing stance is the authentic curiosity to understand the other person's behaviour, combined with the uncertainty and modesty that we can never do this with absolute certainty. We have described how fragile the mentalizing process can be in each of us, and how quickly we can switch between effective and ineffective mentalizing.

The next chapter will go into the latter in more detail. We discuss the main manifestations of ineffective mentalizing and its effect on relationships between people.

3

The vulnerability of mentalizing

In the previous chapter, we described mentalizing as a process that goes on in our heads all the time, implicitly or explicitly. However, mentalizing is not always effective. Everyone regularly loses his or her ability to mentalize properly. This can lead to a relapse into prementalizing modes or states. These prementalizing modes are usually at the root of problems in relationships. They can also cause severe symptoms or psychopathology.

Ineffective or poor mentalizing can have three typical expressions. In the first form, we are too sure that what we think and feel is true. We call this the psychic equivalence mode. In the second form, experiences or intentions are inferred from tangible evidence or actions. We call this the teleological mode. The third form is characterized by a disconnection between the inner and outer world. This form, in which too little contact is made with feelings and needs, is called the pretend mode. In this chapter, we will discuss these three typical prementalizing modes. We will also show you how to recognize them, and the effect of these modes on yourself and relationships with others.

Prementalizing modes:
- Psychic equivalence mode: what I feel or think is the truth.
- Teleological mode: I rely solely on physical actions and tangible evidence.
- Pretend mode: I have no contact with my emotional world.

Psychic equivalence: What I feel or think is true

In Chapter 2, we discussed that effective mentalizing is characterized by uncertainty. It seems contradictory: good mentalizing allows us to 'read' others so that relationships become predictable, and at the same time good mentalizing involves recognizing that we can never know others with certainty. That uncertainty has to do with something very fundamental that we have to learn as children, namely that we all have our own mind. I have thoughts, feelings,

The Power of Mentalizing. Joost Hutsebaut, Liesbet Nijssens, and Miriam van Vessem, Oxford University Press.

and needs, and they don't have to be the same as the thoughts, feelings, and needs of others. *I am distinct from others.* This means that you may experience our contact differently than I do. Maybe I thought you liked something, when you actually experienced it as painful. Recognizing that the other person has a separate mind is therefore quite deterring. It means I am not sure anymore that what I think about you is right. But also, the other way around: it means that you are not sure what I need. Recognizing that others have a different mind can evoke much uncertainty and sometimes even frustration. It is a quality that we must develop. That quality goes hand in hand with the development of individuality: I am someone, a 'self', that is different from your 'self'.

In the psychic equivalence mode, this 'uncertainty' is lost. We are thrown back to more primitive parts of our brain and make almost automatic assumptions about ourselves and others. For example, we fall into value judgements or first impressions, or attribute negative intentions to ourselves or others. In those cases, you immediately make assumptions about the other person's intentions, instead of calmly thinking about it. You no longer recognize the boundary between your own mind and the mind of the other person: I *know* what you think and feel.

That's what we see with Jasmine and Vera.

Jasmine and Vera
Jasmine has a relationship with Vera. In general, they are very happy together, but sometimes they have heated arguments. Jasmine is very precise and Vera can be sloppy. For Jasmine it is important that everything has a fixed place and she also expects Vera to take this into consideration: it is a small effort to put something back in the same place after using it. For Vera, this is less important, and she tends to forget this instruction.

Last night Vera borrowed Jasmine's car, but she forgot to put the key back in the key box. When Jasmine wants to leave for work the next morning, she cannot find them. She is worried that she will be late and is angry that Vera has failed to keep their agreement again. Vera is still sleeping when Jasmine storms in and wakes her up in a fury: 'Now you've lost my stuff for the umpteenth time. You always do that even though you know that I hate that! You don't have the slightest respect for me. You never take into account what I ask! You only think of yourself. If I'm late for work, it will be your fault!' Vera, who had imagined the morning differently, bites back at her: 'They're just in my purse, nag,' and turns around. Jasmine angrily stomps downstairs, empties Vera's bag in the middle of the hall, picks up the key from the floor and slams the door shut behind her.

Recognizable, right? Jasmine is in a hurry and in danger of being late for work. She ends up in a state in which her thoughts become undifferentiated. She knows that Vera has lost her keys. It's the same old story. She can never depend on her. Fortunately, Vera was sober enough (or still too sleepy) not to respond to these accusations. You can imagine it doesn't take much for such an interaction to get out of hand. Think back to Eric and Nathan from the previous chapter. In both examples, ineffective mentalizing is characterized by firm but erroneous assumptions—they 'know' what is going on inside the other person. Jasmine, Eric, and Nathan are in a state of mind that we call 'psychic equivalence' mode. That is, what is in my psyche (what I think and feel) is equal to what is happening in reality.

We all regularly relapse into such a state of psychic equivalence, some easier than others. Some people may experience the world as scary, for example, because they have experienced a lot of insecurity in relationships. We will come back to this in Chapter 5. When this is the case, someone may fall back into psychic equivalence very often or quickly. After all, in such a state the world becomes clearer and more predictable: black is black and white is white, always is always, and never is never. I know you want to take advantage of me, so I turn you down. In psychic equivalence mode, one makes the world simpler and clearer than it actually is. It is not helpful in achieving well-attuned contact with others, but maybe it sometimes helps to give yourself some clarity about the world.

Psychic equivalence can occur when you are very stressed, although this is not a condition. Sometimes people can have fixed beliefs that they don't want to question for whatever reason: men don't have feelings; children should not be spoiled; if you don't immediately show who's the boss in a class, they'll walk all over you; women always cry, that's why they can't reach the top.

> Do you know when you relapse into psychic equivalence? When was the last time that happened and what happened? What made you so emotional or stressed that you lost your effective mentalizing? Or are you aware of beliefs that you don't question enough?

From the above, we can infer how to recognize a state of psychic equivalence. The core is: what I think and feel is true. If someone makes statements that are too absolute or with too little uncertainty, this can be a signal of psychic equivalence. Typical words are: always, never, everyone, nobody, words that make reality too simple. Another signal is when someone uses clinchers: 'I can't help it; I just have a short fuse.' When you yourself are a target of psychic equivalence, you notice that you are being given a label that does not (completely) fit, for example: 'You don't like me, I can see it in your eyes.' Someone no longer doubts the truth of his or her statements.

In fact, in the psychic equivalence mode, a person lays claim to feelings, thoughts, opinions, and beliefs: I know the truth. There is no room for another perspective, opinion, or truth. The effect of psychic equivalence on the interaction can be felt in the example of Jasmine and Vera: it is so easy to get caught up in a conversation in which you don't reach each other, in a hopeless discussion. Psychic equivalence tempts you to do so: you want to refute the other person's beliefs. 'It's not true what you say, I like you.' 'No, you're lying, you just don't say what you really think!' 'I do …' Or you try to give reasonable arguments, but they don't help to change the conviction of the other person. Psychic equivalence often leads to frustration, misunderstanding, and irritation. You can imagine that vulnerable people who are often in a state of psychic equivalence live in a world in which they very often encounter misunderstanding and in which they feel unheard.

Teleological mode: First see, then believe

We cannot perceive trust, honesty, disappointment, love, and other 'mental' phenomena directly. They are neither visible nor tangible. We have to derive and interpret them. That does not always provide certainty and guidance. If you could not rely on the love or commitment of others in the past, it is deterring to have trust in these in your current life and relationships. The teleological mode takes us back to the support we often looked for in the world when we were little children: Mom is only present mentally when she is present physically. Or—When I bleed, I am in pain. If I have a fever, I am sick. If I'm on the penalty seat, I'm naughty. In this way, a child succeeds in organizing and understanding the world. Characteristic of the teleological mode is that something tangible must be done or present in order for something mental or emotional to be experienced. In a teleological mode, there is (apparent) clarity. The justification of invisible mental states is sought in visible things and actions. Falling back into teleological mode is a way of simplifying our understanding of the world by making it dependent—as with young children—on visible things and actions. 'If my partner gives me flowers, it's a sign of his love for me.' Or, 'It's only natural to feel hurt if your birthday is forgotten.'

Elizabeth and Ava

Elizabeth has just become a mother. She recently enrolled her daughter Ava in daycare. Elizabeth would have preferred to stay at home to take care of Ava herself, but she has to go back to work. She finds it difficult to trust that others will care for Ava as well as she does herself. When Elizabeth picks up her daughter from daycare, she wants to know exactly how Ava's day went. She expects a detailed written report from the caregivers daily: How long did Ava sleep, how many cc did she drink, how often was her diaper changed, how often did she cry and for what reason, and was she easy to comfort? The report is often less extensive than Elizabeth would like. At those times, she can be very disappointed. Elizabeth needs this information to feel that Ava is well taken care of.

One day one of the caregivers is sick. The other colleagues have worked very hard all day, but they did not manage to write the daily report. When Elizabeth picks up Ava, the carers apologize for this and briefly tell her something about the day. Elizabeth becomes angry and finds this neglect unacceptable: 'If you can't even bother to write something in her report, how am I supposed to be able to trust that you take good care of Ava? If this happens again, I'll find another daycare!'

Elizabeth does not mentalize well in this example. Only concrete, tangible actions by the caregivers give her the confidence that they have good intentions with Ava. Seeing is believing. Maybe she's too anxious to let go of Ava and to trust that others are also able to take good care of her. As a result, she is dependent on visible evidence as signs of commitment and care. Absence of this evidence confirms in Elizabeth's mind that Ava is not being properly cared for. There is no room for the realization that the time that the caregivers need to write their report cannot be spent on the actual care of Ava. Even though Elizabeth only wants her daughter to be well taken care of, the fear she experiences makes her lose the attunement with the other person and makes her unable to realize what it is like for the caregivers to be approached in such a compelling way.

What would the daycare staff think and feel about Elizabeth's reaction? It might not have been possible to write something, but they knew what the day had been like for Ava and explained this verbally. They may find Elizabeth's accusations unjustified and unfair. Also, they may not understand why Elizabeth reacts so strongly: 'Can't she see how hard we work?' It could be that they feel the urge to prove that they are really involved and able to take good care of Ava. They may feel pressured to try even harder or write more extensive reports for Elizabeth than for other parents. Not because they find this necessary, but because they feel the demand from Elizabeth and hope to keep her happy.

In the teleological mode, there is usually a need (happiness, love, understanding, being seen), but it takes concrete action or physical evidence to feel that that need is being met. Something tangible has to be done or present in order to experience something mental or emotional, for example: 'When I get flowers from my partner, I feel that he loves me.' But also: a certain experience (e.g., worthlessness) can only change through physical actions (e.g., getting a compliment). The desired action that is required to have or change a mental experience usually manifests itself in a demanding appeal to others (see Elizabeth's example), but this is not always the case. Think, for example, about the neighbour who says that she will only be happy once she has had her stomach surgery and is slim again. Her happiness is determined by the action of the stomach surgery; until this surgery has taken place, she will consider herself too fat and ugly, and will continue to feel unhappy.

Numerous examples of the teleological mode can be found in everyday life. For example, consider the woman who expects her partner to say he loves her at least five times a day. The proof of love must come through a tangible action: *telling* that he loves her. Or that one client who can only feel that his therapist is involved when extra sessions are planned. Or the partner who demands that the household be divided equally, in order to feel that there is an equal relationship. The examples may also make it clear that some of the aspects we associate with this teleological mode are not necessarily bad. It is not wrong to expect that the other person in a relationship will also do things for you, such as giving a bouquet on your birthday. It is often nice when your desires are answered by deeds. It does become a problem when only actions and deeds suffice as proof, or when an intention is linked to (the lack of) actions: the partner who does not send messages is out to hurt his wife. Or the therapist who does not want to schedule an extra session is not involved. She doesn't care if the client feels bad.

The effect of the teleological mode is often that you feel pressured or manipulated. That you no longer feel the freedom to do what you want or to be who you want to be. The GP must turn his patient inside out one more time to prove that he takes his complaints seriously; the care provider feels compelled to extend the appointment in order not to disappoint the client. Often the teleological mode has another effect: the other person becomes frustrated and irritated: 'What more do I have to do to prove that I am faithful and will not cheat on you?' 'How many times does Mommy have to tell you how much she loves you?' The effect of the teleological mode on the other person can also be a counter-reaction: the other intentionally does not do what the other demands, for example to protect their own autonomy. The other person only reacts to the behaviour and there is no longer any attention for the underlying need.

Consider whether you can recognize examples of the teleological mode in your personal or professional life. Are there things your partner does that you interpret as proof of his love for you? What happens if your best friend or close colleague forgets your birthday? Does that say something about his or her involvement with you? What is your emotional need behind it?

And vice versa, do you ever do things in a certain way to convince the other person of your good intentions or involvement? Think of examples where you felt compelled to do something that you actually didn't feel okay with, just to prove your good intentions to the other person. Think about its effect on you and try to see what emotional need might be behind the other person's demand.

Pretend mode: No contact with the emotional world

In the examples so far, the following applies mainly: 'What I feel or think is real' (psychic equivalence mode: example of Jasmine and Vera, and of Eric and Nathan), and: 'What I see is real' (teleological mode: example of Elizabeth). You could say that the experiences of Eric, Jasmine, and Elizabeth are too real. In addition, ineffective mentalizing can manifest itself in experiences that are too unreal. In those cases, people are in pretend mode, as in the following example from Rachel and Lisa:

Rachel and Lisa
Rachel is invited by her team leader Lisa for an interview. Lisa is worried about Rachel because she seems a bit absent lately. Instead of drinking coffee in the morning or having lunch with the rest of the team—something she was always up for in the past—she goes for a walk or works during the break. Her productivity at work also seems to be declining somewhat, while previously she was always enthusiastic about her work. She hardly recognizes the cheerful Rachel from the past and she wonders what is going on.
   Lisa asks Rachel how she is doing. She tells Rachel that she has the impression that Rachel is more withdrawn and less enthusiastic about her work lately and that she has been wondering whether there's something wrong with

Rachel. Rachel doesn't seem to recognize her supervisor's concerns. She does acknowledge that she has been spending more time alone and that lately she hasn't been as productive as before, but you can't always be on top of things. She is not sure if there's anything wrong, but she does feel a bit empty sometimes. At times, she disconnects from her colleagues, especially now that the topic during the coffee breaks is always the upcoming company party. All employees are invited along with their partners and there is plenty of speculation about what the party will be like. Everyone is up for it, but Rachel isn't. She's not sure who to invite. She doesn't have a partner. At home she often goes for a walk alone in the woods because that is healthy and helps her get her thoughts in order.

Halfway through the conversation Lisa notices that she is not really listening anymore. She pulls herself together and asks Rachel whether she's worried about the company party. Rachel answers that she is not. She says that, of course, she is a bit apprehensive, but that is normal in these situations. She figures she can always bring a friend to the party. Two colleagues, also without a partner, have indicated that they will simply take someone else with them. Rachel then talks some more about the company party. After half an hour they end the conversation.

Afterwards, when Lisa thinks about the conversation with Rachel, she can't quite remember what they talked about. She realizes she doesn't have an idea how Rachel really feels.

> When you read this example, do you get a sense of how Rachel really feels? Perhaps not... Do you have any idea why we get so little insight into Rachel? Have you ever experienced something like this yourself?

In this example, we see how Rachel's feelings are almost elusive. There is a conversation between the manager and Rachel, but we don't connect with Rachel. How anxious is she really about the company party? What is it really like for her to feel disconnected from her colleagues? In this example, Rachel is not consciously keeping her supervisor at bay, for example, because she is ashamed of her feelings or because she is afraid of Lisa's reaction. In the way Rachel is talking, she seems to be disconnected from herself and her own feelings. It's as if Rachel isn't talking about herself, but rather telling a story about herself. Perhaps Rachel is not in touch with what she is experiencing at that moment, but it could also be that she is often 'alienated' from herself. Maybe she often feels empty, disinterested, and passive. And possibly, as a result, there is nothing that really 'fuels' her, nothing that could make her passionate.

In pretend mode, words and feelings are disconnected. People talk 'about' themselves, not from 'within' themselves. They tell stories without really connecting with their emotional meaning. Sometimes they also feel flat and empty about it. As with the psychic equivalence and teleological modes, elements of this pretend mode are common to everyone. We daydream, wander off, and listen to someone without really thinking about it. We talk about our experiences on autopilot. We explain our behaviour too rationally. The pretend mode only becomes a problem when we can no longer connect with our own feelings or those of others. Sometimes literally nothing is felt anymore, not even physically. An extreme form of pretend mode is dissociation. Contact with the outside world is completely lost, and physical pain reactions (e.g., during self-harm) are also absent. Conversely, a lack of contact with one's own emotional world can also give rise to numerous physical pain complaints, often without a medical explanation.

The pretend mode usually has the effect that the other person drifts off. The story being told does not really interest. We are in danger of getting bored and can't really sympathize. In that sense, it is not surprising that the manager is in danger of losing her attention. You hardly realize what the conversation is really about. Take Lisa: she can't quite remember the conversation, perhaps because it was also difficult for her to get in touch with what was being said. The effect on Rachel is that she will receive little understanding, support, and recognition. There are hardly any feelings for others to try and understand. There is a great risk of others letting her be distant or distancing themselves from her and, like Rachel herself, ignoring the underlying burden.

Fundamental differences between the three modes

In the psychic equivalence or teleological mode, the tension is usually (but not necessarily) high: you are so convinced of your own perspective that you cannot tolerate differences in perspective, creating a constant threat of getting into a discussion (psychic equivalence mode). Or there is a compelling need that can only be fulfilled by concrete actions, which makes the other walk on eggshells (teleological mode). Incomprehension and blame are lurking. In the pretend mode, on the other hand, the tension is low. The emotional experience is flat. The other person does participate in the conversation, but neither is encouraged to think about what is happening to themselves, to the other and between each other. The psychic equivalence and teleological modes provide too few (emotional) barriers ('You have to think, feel, and do what I think, feel, and want. You are no longer allowed to be yourself'), while the pretend mode creates too much emotional barriers: you don't get in touch with your own feelings and the other doesn't get in touch with you.

People often have a 'preferred mode' that they fall into when they regress to prementalizing modes. That doesn't mean they don't fall into other modes as well. For example, someone can be in a pretend mode, but if something happens that affects the person in question, he or she can end up in psychic equivalence mode, in which contact with the underlying feelings is restored and the emotional world suddenly becomes too intense or too much. Think, for example, of an adolescent who behaves mostly detached, but suddenly becomes very indignant, angry, or emotional. Or someone who, with great emotion, tells his story about the death of his father, about how life will never be the same again, but a week later, when you ask how things are going, talks about the event in a very unemotional way. In clinical practice, we encounter this more often. Because the range in which clients are able to mentalize well is usually not that large. Either clients slip into a psychic equivalence or teleological mode—where their tension is high, feelings intense, and where they can be impulsive and demanding—or they are in a pretend mode—where they are detached and feel empty. Subjectively, they then experience either fear and engulfment, or flatness and emptiness.

> Do you know what your preferred mode is? Do you tend to become more rigid in your thinking and feeling, or do you tend to rationalize and disconnect from feelings? And how does ineffective mentalizing manifest itself in your spouse, children, or friends? When you think back to certain situations at work that didn't go well, which mode was dominant?
>
> If you work in healthcare, try to find out with your clients what preferred prementalizing mode they have.

Summary

Bad mentalizing can take three typical expressions. In the psychic equivalence mode, we can be too sure that what we think and feel is true. The effect on the relationship is often that there is an escalation and the arguments fall on deaf ears on both sides. In teleological mode, we can only assume or trust something when we see it or when there is tangible evidence. The effect on the relationship is often that coercion and manipulation are experienced. In pretend mode we have too little contact with our feelings and needs. Often the effect on the relationship is that it is difficult to feel a connection, and as a result the other person will find it hard to listen and be supportive. Thus, any kind of bad mentalizing immediately leads to problems in relationships with other people.

Effective mentalizing also develops in relationships, especially with your caregivers, usually your parents. In the following chapters, we discuss attachment and attachment styles (see Chapter 4 on secure attachment, and Chapter 5 on insecure attachment), and how they relate to effective and ineffective mentalizing.

4

Parenting and the formation of attachment bonds

In the previous chapters, we described the importance of the capacity to mentalize in order to be able to engage in pleasant and understanding relationships. Mentalizing is a capacity that we need to develop. The foundation for this development is made in the first years of life or perhaps even earlier.

> If you have children of your own, can you remember how you and your partner fantasized about what your son or daughter would be like before they were born? If you don't have children, maybe you've thought about what your child would be like?

Oftentimes children already exist in the minds of their parents before they are born. Parents create a mental picture of what their child will be like. They already give meaning to vague signals. For example, if a child is active in the womb, parents may think they will have their work cut out for them with such a character. Once a child is born, this process continues unabated naturally. A daughter who is looking around not long after giving birth is 'curious' and is 'taking in the world completely'. Parents observe their child, think about him or her, and give meaning to what they see or think they see. Thank goodness . . . After all, babies are helpless. If they were dependent on themselves, they would not survive. They need parents who are attuned to them. Parents who are aware of their physical needs (e.g., hunger) and for their emotional needs (e.g., reassurance or comfort). They need mum or dad to give them the breast or a bottle when they're hungry. They need them to change that pesky wet diaper, or to comfort them when they have cramps.

The Power of Mentalizing. Joost Hutsebaut, Liesbet Nijssens, and Miriam van Vessem, Oxford University Press.
© Joost Hutsebaut, Liesbet Nijssens, Miriam van Vessem 2023. DOI: 10.1093/oso/9780198880677.003.0004

Attachment behaviour

Nature has equipped babies with a unique quality: when they need mum or dad, they can attract their attention with certain behaviours. They start crying or whining, shouting 'Mommy!' when they're a little older, or stretching their arms out. They give parents the signal, 'I need you!' And parents are similarly equipped by nature with a unique quality: they pick up those signals and respond. They give the breast or the bottle, change the diaper, pick up the child, answer the cries. Through these seemingly simple actions, something important arises. Hunger, a wet diaper, and cramps are not experienced as such by a baby. Instead, they experience something like a general unrest, something unpleasant, a tension. Because parents are attuned to their baby's signals and almost automatically translate them into the underlying need—which they then act on—a safe environment is created for the baby. With these simple interventions, parents not only ensure that the baby feels calmer, more comfortable, and more relaxed, but they also answer the call for closeness and give the baby what he or she needs. In these interactions, the foundation for attachment is laid.

Day in and day out, there are dozens, if not hundreds of interactions in which parents are attuned to their child and helping them regulate themselves. If a child is tired, parents put them in a crib or cot and protect them from overstimulation so that they can rest. When a child wakes up and is hungry or has a wet diaper, parents read those signals and give them food or a new diaper. However, if a child is alert and satisfied, they take them on their lap and look at drawings in a booklet together. If they cry because they are tired, overstimulated, or hungry, parents help to bridge the time until sleeping or eating, by appeasing the child or walking around with them. Parents thus help the child to regulate an unpleasant state. And they help to slow down the sometimes-abrupt transitions between playing and crying fiercely in order to make them less abrupt.

The behaviour with which babies 'call' their parents or other caring figures is called attachment behaviour. We all know this behaviour in babies and children, but older children and adults also exhibit attachment behaviour. For example, if you are abroad for a training course and your laptop is stolen, you may not only want to solve this problem practically, but you may also feel the need to call home. Not that your partner can provide you with a replacement laptop immediately, but he or she can help you calm down a bit. And it's just nice to hear or see familiar people in moments of stress.

Secure attachment and emotion regulation

Based on all these small, everyday experiences, a child will develop a picture of what his or her parents are like during the first years of their life. For example, little Charlotte has noticed that mommy comes to investigate when she cries and that she then gets a bottle, or that mommy picks her up and whispers comforting words. Samuel's dad also seems to understand him most of the time, for example because he picks up Samuel and throws him in the air the moment he outstretches his arms. Samuel then laughs out loud. These kinds of experiences allow Charlotte and Samuel to feel safe with their parents. They feel their parents are there when they need them, and that they're having good intentions. We call this secure attachment. The child knows where they can find comfort and help, because they have been able to experience countless times that mum and dad, grandma, and grandpa, and later also the childcare worker or the kindergarten teacher, are there for him or her. If they feel anxious or alone, they will also seek the proximity of these care figures. For example, by being close to mum or grandpa, the child can refuel briefly, and then go back and focus on what they were doing.

> Being securely attached means that you have the expectation that important others, also called attachment figures, will be available and caring when you are anxious, stressed, or tense.

Tess

Tess is three years old and is going to daycare for the first time. She's really looking forward to it. Her parents have been looking forward with Tess to this first day. They've already visited the class when it was empty to take a first look. Tess immediately discovered the doll's corner, and since then she hasn't talked about anything else. She will certainly play in the doll's corner on the first day. However, when dad and Tess arrive at the school, something changes in Tess: the excitement gives way to fear. All those new and unfamiliar faces are pretty scary for her, and all those kids playing make quite a lot of noise. Tess is overwhelmed by all these impressions and suddenly she doesn't know if she wants to be here anymore. She hides behind dad's leg and holds on tightly to his pant leg. Daddy strokes her head and says, 'That's a lot of new faces, aren't they?' Meanwhile, the teacher comes up to them and shakes dad's hand. Dad tells her that Tess was really looking forward to coming to play, but that she seems to find it a bit scary now. The teacher kneels and looks Tess in the eye: 'Hi Tess, I'm Jessica. I understand that you have to get used to this, but I'm sure you will really like it here. What do you like to play with?' Tess looks at dad a little anxiously. Dad tells Jessica that Tess likes to play with dolls and that she has been looking forward to playing in the doll's corner. 'How nice! Come on, I'll show you the doll's corner. Do you see that girl with curly hair? That's Eve, she also likes to play with dolls. You will probably become good friends', Jessica reassures her. She extends her hand to Tess. Tess looks at dad, who gives her an encouraging nod. Carefully she gives Jessica her hand and walks with her to the doll's corner. Halfway there, Tess looks back, and starts to pout. Dad raises his thumb and shouts, 'I'm proud of you, darling! Have fun and see you soon!' The pout starts to turn into a smile.

Tess is anxious in a new and unknown situation: the daycare felt a lot safer without children and with mum and dad there. Realizing that dad will go away and that she will be alone at the big place with all those unfamiliar faces … Tess is used to seeking reassurance from dad when she gets anxious. She has the conviction that when she is afraid, daddy will take care of her, that he will do what is best for her, and that she can trust him. In this example, we see dad do at least three important things: he attunes to her emotion of that moment ('lots of new faces', 'scary'), he helps her gain trust in Jessica (he talks to her and expresses something of how he thinks Tess feels), and he strengthens her self-confidence ('I'm proud of you'). Dad's encouraging look teaches her that it's okay to trust Jessica. This is in accordance with her own feelings, because when Jessica looks at her and smiles sweetly at her, she suddenly becomes a lot less scary. Jessica also seems interested in her and what she likes. Tess feels acknowledged in her fear. Dad and Jessica both show in their reactions that they understand that it is scary for Tess. This makes it possible for Tess to endure the fear and tension and she gradually finds more room to explore. It is quite possible that during the course of the day she will occasionally refuel with Jessica to be able to keep playing, until she feels safe and comfortable enough in this new and scary situation.

This is an example that every toddler or pre-schooler will have to deal with. Try to consider what Tess learns about herself and others in such situations. What effect will such learning experiences have on the trust she has in herself and in others?

Dad helps Tess regulate herself in a new and scary situation. He attunes to what Tess might feel and reflects back to her how he understands her reaction. We call this 'mirroring'.

Mirroring

Mirroring means that the parents (or other caregivers) hold up a kind of mirror to the child, so that in the reaction of the parent the child can better understand what the child feels and experiences. But unlike a real mirror, the reaction of parents does not mirror exactly. Let's clarify that with another example.

> *Julia and Finn*
>
> *Julia is the mother of three-month-old Finn. It's noon and Finn is sleeping in his crib. Usually, he sleeps for a long time and that is why Julia takes the time to quickly do some chores in the house. In her haste, Julia knocks over a vase, which promptly clatters to the ground with a lot of noise. Almost immediately, she hears cries from Finn's room. Julia goes to Finn, picks him up and comforts him: 'My poor boy, did I startle you? Mummy made a lot of noise, didn't she?' She holds him tightly and cradles him while making soothing noises. This calms Finn down and after a few minutes, Julia gently puts him back in his crib.*

Finn starts crying after he wakes up, startled by the noise. Julia picks up this signal ('There's something going on with Finn'), goes to him and comforts him. She does this by picking him up, so that he feels her comfort, but also by addressing him with a gentle and loving intonation in her voice. Julia mentions that Finn may have been startled by the loud noise. She gives words to his experience. But she does more than that. With everything she does, what she says and how she does and says this, she helps Finn to regulate his emotion, which he himself cannot yet handle properly. She reads the feelings behind the crying, shows him that she wants to be there for him and tries to put into words what Finn might feel. This teaches Finn to recognize and handle this uncomfortable feeling within himself. And this is not the only time that Julia does this; she does it many times a day, every day.

Young children are not familiar with emotions such as fear, sadness, anger, and shame. They only know lust/unrest, pleasant/annoying, or tension/relaxation. Feelings are initially very physical: babies have sensations in their body that are pleasant or unpleasant. Those sensations only become feelings when parents name them as such. We refer to physical sensations that lie at the basis of what we call 'feelings' or 'emotions', with the word 'affect'.

What Julia does with Finn is called mirroring or affect mirroring for that reason. In her response to Finn, she mirrors some of the fright or fear she hears in his crying. Julia's mimicry aligns with Finn's emotion, as Julia understands it. If that alignment is correct, we call the reflection congruent. This means that Julia has attuned correctly into the feeling that Finn is experiencing and shows this in her reaction. For example, in a congruent reflection, the facial expression and intonation of the caregiver correspond with what the child himself expresses. The child's experience is then 'correctly' mirrored. Parents almost always do this spontaneously and intuitively. For example, they not only mention the behaviour, but also the experience behind it: 'That seems like an exciting film that you are watching'; 'Is it fun on grandma's lap?'; 'It's not nice when your sister squeezes you like that'. Parents who are aware of their child's actual 'mental states' while interacting with their child, create more safety in the relationship. The child then feels 'known' and 'understood' by his or her parents. In other words, the child feels mentalized.

However, if the mirroring of the caregiver does not match the experience of the child, we speak of incongruent mirroring. Imagine, for example, that Julia had reacted with anger to Finn's crying and had said with some frustration in her voice: 'Stop crying, it wasn't that bad.' Julia may mirror ('It wasn't that bad'), but her rendering doesn't match the experience of Finn, who is upset.

> Do you recognize examples of congruent mirroring in your surroundings? Do you have examples of yourself, for example as a parent, teacher, counsellor? What was the effect on the relationship at that time? Do you see examples of incongruent mirroring around you or in your own history? What would be the consequences of incongruent mirroring?

In addition, it is important that the affect mirroring is 'marked' by the caregiver. Julia marks her mirroring by asking Finn with raised eyebrows and a high voice whether he was startled. In doing so, she makes it clear to Finn that she is not startled herself, but that she is reflecting something from what he has experienced. Marking means: drawing a line, distinguishing between my experience (mind) and your experience (mind). Parents typically do this by a somewhat exaggerated or magnified mimicry, or by a more playful intonation. In doing so, it is made clear that the mirrored feeling belongs to the child and not to the parent or caregiver. Because of the mirroring by Julia, Finn learns that his experience—which initially consists purely of arousal—can be tolerated, can acquire meaning, and can therefore also be regulated. Mummy says she knows and recognizes his feelings, but that it doesn't frighten her and will help him deal with it.

> Notice how quickly people, even without children of their own, adapt their tone of voice, intonation, and language to a baby: they slow down, become more playful, increase their mimicry. Pay attention to the interactions between parents and babies, especially when the baby feels uncomfortable. Do you know of examples in yourself or around you of marked and unmarked mirroring?

> **Features of a good affect mirroring:**
> Congruent: there is similarity between the affect in the child and that which is mirrored by the caregiver.
>
> Marked: in the mirroring it is made clear that it is not the affect of the caregiver that is mirrored, but that of the child.

Secure attachment and the internal working model

Through accurate affect mirroring, children experience their parents in a predictable way: they take his or her needs and feelings seriously, recognize them as important and valuable, and respond to them. As a result, the child develops the expectation that the parents are caring, reliable, and available. These expectations are also referred to as the working model or the blueprint about the parent. A working model in which the child expects that parents are available and caring, is called a secure attachment. In general, securely attached children are mirrored congruently and in a marked way by their parents. Through that mirroring, the child implicitly receives a very important message: parents acknowledge and indicate that there is 'self' in the child, a 'self' that is worth being seen, a 'self' with all kinds of experiences that are allowed to be there. Experiences that cannot simply be 'made to disappear' quickly, but that must be answered and acknowledged, and thus also given meaning and regulated.

What takes place between Julia and Finn is one of dozens of examples of mirroring that Finn experiences every day and one of the thousands of mirror experiences he will acquire in his young life. Of course, Julia doesn't always mirror correctly. You don't have to. Sometimes parents themselves are tired and therefore not congruently attuned to their child, or something happens that causes them to go along with strong emotions without properly marking their own experience. Even the best parents are not constantly able to completely attune to their child's needs. The mere fact that parents engage in a process of looking for attunement, is more important than that the mirroring is always and immediately 'correct'. When a parent notices that there is a 'mismatch' between the child's experience and their own affect mirroring, he or she will look for ways to correct that by again trying to attune to the child. This process determines a child's experience in a relationship. If the child usually has the experience that his emotions are picked up and mirrored in a congruent and marked way, then he himself will become more curious, learn to experience that emotions can acquire meaning and can be regulated, and he will start to experience his inner world as 'safe'. If there is sufficient attunement, the child will include painful moments of being unheard and ununderstood in a wider stream of good experiences. Difficult moments are therefore quickly forgotten. Moreover, parents are not alone. If mum and dad don't manage to connect with the child and they are not sufficiently aware of what it feels and desires, then there's still grandma or granddad, the neighbour, the babysitter, the kindergarten teacher, or the mom or dad of a friend. In a normal, healthy development, children will gain positive experiences through different contacts and relationships, in which they feel seen, heard, and recognized.

While a child initially needs others to get to know, recognize, tolerate, and regulate his or her feelings, they will gradually learn to do this themself: 'It's okay to feel what I feel, and I can use those feelings to better understand myself.' For example, a child may experience that parents are interested in his or her inner world and is not bluntly judged by his or her behaviour. With the help of important others, the child comes to understand why it felt so bad. He or she doesn't learn that it's better to suppress feelings or behaviour, for fear of negative consequences, but begins to understand why it feels so bad and what they need at such a moment, for example, resting in the car when they are tired and overstimulated. In this way, the foundation is laid for how they will deal with emotions and needs. It develops basic scripts for dealing with oneself and others when they need others.

In short, it is important that a child experiences that his or her parents are able to look beyond the actual, concrete behaviour, and that they can give meaning to that behaviour in a correct way based on what is happening in the inner world of the child. If a child experiences that, for the most part, his or her emotions are picked up and mirrored in a congruent and marked way, then it develops a kind of space within itself in which it can look at emotions, give meaning to them, and learn to regulate those emotions.

Influence of inappropriate mirroring on attachment

It becomes problematic when the mirroring is constantly distorted, for example, if the reflection is often unmarked. That would be the case, for example, if Julia started to panic completely from Finn's crying. She would still mirror something, and what she mirrors would even be congruent (both are in a panic), but there would be no distinction (marking) between Finn's experience and that of Julia. Finn's own fear and panic would only increase as a result. If a child is often mirrored in an unmarked way, then the distinction between one's own emotions and those of others fades. Think back for a moment to the psychic equivalence mode, in which there is no longer a boundary between my feelings and your feelings. What I feel is the truth. Fear becomes fear squared. One's own experience cannot be regulated and even increases in intensity. There is a good chance that the young child will be overwhelmed by emotions that make the child even more afraid. His or her experiences then remain unnamed, confusing, and difficult to tolerate and regulate. A child learns that feelings are dangerous and becomes afraid of his or her own inner world. These children will often feel powerless and helpless in handling their own emotions: 'Once I start to feel, there is no end to it and I need others so as not to get completely overwhelmed.' They have little self-confidence and feel very dependent, even if that dependence feels frightening, because others can also get upset by their emotions.

If a child is often mirrored incongruently, it learns that some of its emotional experiences 'are not allowed'. For example, when parents don't mirror fear or sadness as such: 'You're a big boy now, you don't have to cry about that anymore.'

Frequent incongruent mirroring can cause a child to become alienated from a part of his or her emotional world. There is no connection between what is experienced and what is mirrored. Think back for a moment to the pretend mode, which we discussed in Chapter 3: becoming disconnected from one's own emotions. One step further, incongruent mirroring also has an effect on self-image. The child learns that parts of him should not be there: 'When I cry, I exaggerate. I'm a crybaby, a difficult child.' These children often learn to handle their emotions by ignoring them. They have learned that it is better not to lean on others when they feel afraid or sad, because that makes them weak.

The importance of parental mentalizing

For the development of a child, it is important that it feels mentalized. This ensures security in the important relationships it enters. It ensures that children learn to consider their own emotions, connect with them, and that they gain the confidence that they are able to get a grip on their own inner world and that they can regulate their own behaviour in this way. Children need parents to mirror them. This requires parents to be able to mentalize their child. However, this is not always self-evident.

Hazel
Hazel is five years old. Today she and her parents visited an amusement park. It was a very nice day and Hazel was allowed to do everything she wanted. On the way home they pass a supermarket, and mom and dad decide to do some shopping. Hazel disagrees and does not want to. She throws herself on the ground and starts screaming. Tears roll down her cheeks.

Hazel's behaviour can be interpreted in different ways. When Hazel's parents are tired or stressed, their capacity to mentalize may be diminished. Maybe they're thinking, 'Spoiled child! The whole afternoon has revolved around you, we've done everything you wanted, and now you can't even bother to do something we want. Is it really that hard to behave for half an hour?' Dad may get angry and take Hazel under his arm, while she is kicking and screaming harder and harder. Hazel's parents perceive her behaviour very concretely ('Hazel is a spoiled child') and are not able to consider the underlying experience or meaning of her 'spoiled' behaviour. Because of her parents' reaction, Hazel may feel rejected. When Hazel frequently has these kinds of experiences in contact with her parents, she may begin to take over the image that her parents have of her as a difficult and spoiled child.

If Hazel's parents manage to look beyond the visible behaviour and reflect on her underlying experience, the subsequent interaction may be very different. Effective mentalizing ensures that the parents, for example, realize that Hazel is tired of all the impressions after a long day in the amusement park. They understand that at this moment, a visit to the supermarket may be too much to ask, even if it is something that needs to be done. Mum could then ask dad to wait in the car with Hazel, while she quickly gets the groceries. Dad may realize that getting angry would only exacerbate the situation and that it's important to stay calm. He may feel that he is also stressed by the situation and ashamed of the looks from passers-by. Both mum and dad try to empathize with how Hazel feels, and they think about the meaning of her behaviour. They tune in to their daughter's underlying needs and thus help her to better regulate herself.

This example shows that often parents only manage to react in such a sensitive way when they first are able to mentalize about themselves. If dad can consider his feelings of shame and anger while Hazel lies kicking and screaming on the floor, this will help him to respond better to the situation. On the one hand, this will make him realize, for example, that acting from anger and shame towards Hazel may not help her to calm down. On the other hand, this will also give him more mental space to keep thinking about Hazel and what she needs. If a parent can no longer mentalize well about his or her own emotions, this increases the chance that he or she can no longer properly mirror the child's emotions. Parents then quickly fall into incongruent mirroring ('Don't be so annoying, spoiled child!'), perhaps because they cannot adequately regulate their own tension, evoked by the behaviour of their child.

Sometimes it is claimed that parents who have been traumatized in their childhood pass this on to their children. However, research shows that this is by no means a law set in stone. What is important is that parents can continue to mentalize about themselves in difficult situations, for example, when their child experiences a lot of stress. When you, as a parent, experience intense negative emotions, which can become dangerous to yourself, then you can lose your own mentalizing ability when your child is very upset. But this doesn't have to happen. Much depends on whether parents are at peace with their own history, including sometimes particularly painful experiences, and whether they can mentalize about it.

> Do you have feelings you find difficult to experience? Feelings you are judgemental about? Are there any needs or desires that you'd rather not acknowledge? Can you acknowledge all your feelings and needs?

Everyone has their own attachment history. We all have our own experiences from our early relationships that are strengthened or corrected in our later relationships. This attachment history partly determines whether parents have an eye for their child's mental states and whether they can continue to mentalize about themselves when it is 'difficult'. The better parents are able to think about what the child thinks, feels, and desires, the better they can respond to his or her behaviour—even if it is perceived as disturbing. They reflect on what their child's behaviour means, form an image of the inner world that lies behind the behaviour and respond better to the needs and needs of the child.

Before concluding this chapter, let's clarify three more things. First, adequate mirroring does not mean that parents should not set limits to behaviour. Of course, Hazel's parents are allowed to put a stop to inappropriate behaviour. However, it is important that it does not stop there: 'You have to stop shouting and crying now. I understand you are tired and that it might all be a bit too much. We're going to do these groceries, then we'll drive home together and you can rest in the car.' Secondly, parents do not always have to be accurate immediately when mirroring. It is more important that they continue to look for the right attunement, that they remain flexible. This means that parents remain open to other interpretations, that they can acknowledge that what they first thought may not be entirely correct, and that they remain curious. For some parents, that's easier than for others. A woman who is already insecure about herself will probably become more insecure as a mother when she notices that she is not able to immediately calm down her child. A man who quickly feels rejected may also experience this when his son mainly turns to his mother and rejects him. Especially when parents have unpleasant attachment experiences themselves, it can be difficult to tolerate if that scenario repeats itself in relationship with their own child. If their child behaves annoyingly, it can affect a parent in such a way that the ability to mentalize about themselves in contact with the child is negatively affected. As a result, mentalizing about the child will also be made more difficult, which can lead to incongruent or unmarked mirroring. Thirdly, there is no ready-made skill that allows parents to learn to tune in well with their child. Where being strict at bedtime reassures one child, it can actually increase the tension in the other child. And where one child likes to be taken on his lap when crying, another might like to be left alone for a while. The art of parenting lies in the constant attunement to the unique needs of each child at every moment. Mentalizing is the vulnerable compass that parents have at their disposal on this quest, but for some of them it is—partly because of their own attachment history—complicated to keep the right course. A reassuring thought is that no parent is always right. And that's not a bad thing at all: when children are mirrored in a congruent way and marked frequently enough, they develop the secure attachment they need to grow into resilient adult individuals.

Summary

Parents who mirror the internal experiences they pick up on in their child in a congruent and marked way, gradually teach their son or daughter to regulate themselves, not only by directing his or her behaviour, but above all by better understanding the emotions, intentions, and expectations behind them. The child experiences that it is safe to discover his or her own inner world. Because the child feels safe in relation to their caregivers, it also develops confidence, especially the confidence that others can understand what it needs. In this way, the child learns more and more about the social world around him or her, and forms an image of themselves and others as involved and reliable. In addition, parents give their child the message that it is 'someone', a 'self' who wants, finds, feels, and desires. This is how the child develops a unique sense of self. The security that the child experiences also increases the confidence that it has in itself: it dares to rely more and more on what it feels and thinks and on how it interprets the world around it. All these experiences contribute to the development of secure attachment and then also the own ability to mentalize. In the next chapter, we will go deeper into situations in which parents do not manage to continue to mentalize effectively for various reasons.

5

Insecure attachment

If parents are vulnerable or end up in complex living conditions, this can have a major impact on children's attachment development. Think of parents who are depressed and therefore unresponsive. Or of parents who live in poverty, who themselves suffer from trauma or loss, or whose own caregivers had poor mentalizing abilities, and as a result have little contact with their own inner world and that of others. Such parents can temporarily or continuously give little attention to the internal world of their child, draw conclusions too quickly (without remaining curious) or become overwhelmed when their child is upset. Sometimes it is also more difficult to mentalize about a child due to predisposition or (medical) problems: these children may be constantly very tense and restless, or they cry a lot. These children can put even the best mentalizing parents to the test.

> As a parent, do you remember moments or periods when you just 'couldn't do it'? Maybe you were tired or there were other things going on that prevented you from tuning in to your child?

Due to all kinds of circumstances, children can miss the experience that they can rely on caregivers to help them know and handle inner experiences, thoughts, and feelings. The child experiences insecurity in relationships and will try to find his own way to deal with this insecurity. They develop different working models about themselves and the availability of others than their securely attached peers. In this chapter, we discuss the three insecure attachment styles that this lack of a safe haven can result in: anxious-ambivalent, avoidant, and disorganized.

The Power of Mentalizing. Joost Hutsebaut, Liesbet Nijssens, and Miriam van Vessem, Oxford University Press.
© Joost Hutsebaut, Liesbet Nijssens, Miriam van Vessem 2023. DOI: 10.1093/oso/9780198880677.003.0005

Anxious-ambivalent attachment

If children are not able to trust their attachment figures to be there for them, or when they are scared to trust themselves, then they can start clinging to their care persons. The following example illustrates this.

Michelle and Abigail
Michelle became a mother a bit later in life than average. She has always been afraid that she wouldn't be good enough for her child. She didn't have a very good childhood herself and wanted to do better than her own mother. When her daughter Abigail was born, it made her very insecure. She could get upset when Abigail cried for too long and she couldn't comfort her. Abigail only had to make a sound and Michelle was already at her cradle. Her partner often told her to relax more.

When Abigail started school, things were very difficult. She cried often and for a long time, Michelle had to stay with her the whole time until the teacher took over from her. Michelle hated that. When she'd come to pick up her daughter from school, Abigail could be very angry and sometimes she even hit Michelle.

When Michelle meets up with friends who also have children, she notices that Abigail often stays on her lap the whole time and does not like to play with the other children. Secretly, Michelle likes that. It feels nice to feel needed. At the same time, she realizes that it would be better if Abigail would be a bit more independent.

There is a different interaction pattern between Michelle and Abigail than between Julia and Finn (see Chapter 4). Abigail is not really able to stand on her own two feet. She always needs an attachment figure, mother, or teacher. She often stays with her mother and hardly explores the world on her own. She lacks the self-confidence to do so. Abigail is anxious and dependent on another person. There are actually too few boundaries between Michelle and Abigail. Abigail needs Michelle, and maybe the other way around. When Abigail is upset, Michelle easily gets upset as well.

Maybe Michelle doesn't mentalize sufficiently about herself when Abigail is upset: she is unable to regulate herself, she also becomes anxious and panicky, and is no longer able to mirror the experiences of Abigail. As a result, Abigail's emotions are insufficiently mentalized: it is 'scary' to be afraid. If Abigail is afraid, for example when she has to go to school and a new situation has to be mastered there, she shows a lot of attachment behaviour to get mum or the teacher to stay with her. She is too attached and in stressful situations her attachment is too strongly activated as a way to regulate her own tension. At the same time, the relationship between Abigail and Michelle is 'ambivalent': Abigail is too afraid to be alone and needs Michelle, but when Michelle is too present and too caring, Michelle's presence also becomes suffocating and Abigail pushes her away again. After all, she wants to be able to do it herself. But when Michelle is too far, she becomes too anxious and wants Michelle near again. This pattern of insecure attachment is therefore called anxious-ambivalent.

This attachment pattern often characterizes one's relations later in life. People with this attachment style tend to be more anxious and dependent on others. They lack self-confidence and therefore rely strongly on attachment figures, such as parents and a partner. They are often vulnerable to relapses in the psychic equivalence mode: their feelings are dangerous, quickly become intense and too 'real'. They have experienced too little demarcation between their own inner world and the outside world. In situations where they are tense or stressed as an adult, they often show a lot of attachment behaviour.

Avoidant attachment

Anxious-ambivalent children cling very tightly to their attachment figures. In addition, there are also children who seem to care very little about their attachment figures. It looks like they're going their own way and don't need anyone. This attachment style, which we call avoidant, is another way to deal with perceived insecurity in the attachment relationships.

Daisy and Marco
Daisy has a demanding job. She comes from a family of go-getters. She knows she's not very good with emotions. She doesn't know how to deal with them. She thinks problems are there to be solved. She has a son, Marco, who seems to have adopted this attitude from her, he goes his own way and can play on his own for a long time. Marco also seemed to have no problem on the first day of school. He just went into the school, walked to the corner where the cars were, and started playing. When Daisy came to pick him up, he barely looked up. He seemed to like it at school. Daisy wasn't sure if she should be proud or not. It also felt like he didn't need her that much.

Daisy and Marco have a completely different relationship. As the relationship between Michelle and Abigail was too intertwined, too intense, the contact between Daisy and Marco is too distant and almost impersonal. Marco hardly asks for any care, and certainly not for his emotional needs. He may have learned that he would not get a response from Daisy: no need to cry, just get on with it. He avoids closeness and intense contact. Where the attachment of Abigail is too finely adjusted and is activated again and again, Marco switches it off during stress. Does that mean Marco is as calm as he looks? No, we know from research that the physical stress in these children is equally high. Only they don't 'feel' it. They don't connect with these physical sensations.

Probably Marco was not sufficiently mirrored congruently. He may often have experienced that when he was afraid or sad, the mirroring was something like, 'Don't be like that, just keep going!' As a result, he has little connection with these emotions of sadness and fear—he does not mentalize well about them. Marco may have started to think: I am exaggerating when I feel so weak and vulnerable. He may also remain avoidant as an adult. Maybe he has less need for intense, emotionally close relationships. He is emotionally detached and will more often fall back into the pretend mode. He has experienced that he has to rely mainly on himself to solve problems and has little confidence that others can help him with that. Marco won't easily ask for help as an adult, either. In life, you eventually have to do it yourself. It's not easy to get close to Marco.

> We have described the cases of Abigail and Marco as somewhat stereotypical to make them recognizable. In reality, everyone somewhere tends to fall back on one of these styles, even if you are basically securely attached. In which of the two styles do you recognize yourself the most? What is your need when you are under pressure? How does this affect your relationships?

Disorganized attachment

Abigail and Marco have a clear strategy when they are stressed: Abigail clings to mum, and Marco goes his own way. Their behaviour is organized and follows a clear script. This is not the case with some other children. They don't have a clear strategy. Therefore, in those cases we speak of disorganized attachment.

Patty and Sophia
Patty had a traumatic childhood. She was emotionally neglected and sexually abused. She is in a relationship with a man who has a lot of mental health problems himself. Patty wanted a child in order to start a new life. She hoped

that the birth of Sophia would also make her partner calmer and happier. She was completely wrong. The birth overwhelmed her. It felt like all the feelings and memories that were stored away came back with a vengeance. When Sophia cries, it evokes the pain of her own loneliness in her youth. When she has to take care of her, seeing her naked daughter evokes the fear of her child-hood abuse.

Patty tries to keep her head up with all her might. She is often mentally ab-sent. At those times she tries to think and feel nothing. Sometimes this doesn't work. Then the crying and whining of Sophia hurts in her head and stomach. And sometimes she gives her a slap to make it stop. She feels guilty about that. Sophia is clearly confused. She needs her mother sometimes, but at the same time she doesn't know how she will react when she calls her. On the first day of school, she shuffles into the classroom, she looks at Patty, wants to go to her, but stays put. She seems to freeze, not knowing if she wants to walk into the classroom or stay with mum, so she ends up doing nothing. She is confused and paralysed.

Sophia has no strategy to deal with fear or tension, like on the first day of school. She wants to go to Patty but freezes when she wants to. Why is she freezing? Perhaps because she has learned that Patty's reactions are very un-predictable. Mum is sometimes there for her, but she might as well react com-pletely differently. Or she may not respond at all. Sometimes she might give Sophia love, sometimes a slap, and sometimes she ignores her.

Having a disorganized attachment style means that there is no clear pat-tern in the attachment behaviour. These children long for care and security, but at the same time cannot tolerate the care. In turn, they sometimes become very affectionate and at other times angry when the attachment figure says or does something sweet. Often these children have had traumatic experiences in the relationships with their caregivers: for comfort and support, they de-pend on the same caregivers who harm them at other times. They experience a lot of unpredictability and get caught up in their uncertainty, so that there is no strategy that helps in situations of anxiety and stress.

A disorganized attachment style often arises because attachment fig-ures exhibit abrupt and unpredictable behaviour. The normal interac-tion is broken: dad suddenly becomes very angry; mummy suddenly starts screaming for no apparent reason. Often this indicates severe deficiencies in parents' ability to mentalize about themselves. In the abovementioned ex-ample, we see that Patty shows this unpredictable behaviour when she cares for Sophia. If Sophia experiences this unpredictable behaviour more often, then caregivers become very unsafe for her.

Table 5.1 The different attachment styles in stressful situations

Attachment styles	Child's behaviour under stress
Secure attachment	Seek the proximity of caregivers, but when they feel safe, they also go on a journey of discovery on their own.
Anxious-ambivalent attachment	Clings to (strange) care figures, discover too little themselves.
Avoidant attachment	Withdraws into themselves, goes exploring alone.
Disorganized attachment	Don't know what to do, expresses different and often conflicting needs, are confused.

What does Sophia learn about herself and others? Sophia doesn't learn that she can trust herself. Nor does she learn that she can trust others. In her later relationships with others, this can translate into unpredictable behaviour, for example into patterns of attraction and repulsion. From research, we know that children with disorganized attachment patterns are very vulnerable to developing serious mental health problems.

A summary of how the child behaves under stress, depending on its attachment style, is provided in Table 5.1.

Research shows that attachment styles can change over the course of a human life. Undoubtedly, the experiences we gain in the relationships with our primary care figures form an important basis, but around them there are even more people, such as grandparents and teachers. In addition, we develop a whole series of other relationships over the course of our lives. New experiences can change existing attachment styles. People continue to develop throughout their lives.

Summary

In this chapter, we discussed the three main forms of insecure attachment: anxious-ambivalent, avoidant, and disorganized attachment. We outlined the characteristic experiences these children have, the strategies they use in scary or stressful situations, and their effects on the confidence these children develop in themselves and in others. In our discussion, we made reality a little more orderly and simpler than it is. In reality, these three categories are not so clearly distinguishable from each other. Nor is the distinction with secure attachment always so clear. In addition, children can be more securely attached to one attachment figure than to another.

Also, we must not forget that an attachment style can change in the course of a lifetime. In the first chapters, we have described what mentalizing is, how it develops, and how it is related to attachment. In the next chapter, we will focus on the important role that mentalizing plays in our ability to learn from others.

6

Epistemic trust

In previous chapters, we discussed the relationship between mentalizing and attachment. In this chapter, we add a third element: learning from others. Or rather: epistemic trust, the trust in others that underlies one's willingness to accept knowledge from others. Together with the first two concepts, epistemic trust forms a triangle of interdependence. In this chapter, we will elaborate on how learning from others relates to the other two concepts.

It is almost unimaginable what a child has to learn to function in modern society. Learning to eat with a knife and fork, drink from a glass, get dressed, tie your shoelaces, walk, talk, cycle, consider others, play together, and read. Suppose you had to learn everything by yourself ... figure out what a spoon is for or how to tie your shoelaces. Let alone who you are and what you are good at. Fortunately, there is a much more efficient way of learning, namely from *others*. Children learn a lot from their parents. Parents give them practical skills, such as handling spoons and tying shoelaces, but they also learn about themselves and others. Children learn from parents who they are, by seeing themselves through their eyes, and how other people usually interact with them. People acquire by far the most knowledge from others: we therefore speak of *social learning*. For a lifetime, continuous learning is important to further refine and change what we already know about ourselves and the world. This all sounds obvious, and we often don't realize that learning from others is actually quite complex.

Laura and Liam
Liam is thirteen. He has been going to high school for a year now. His parents notice that they have less control over him. Sometimes they catch him lying. He recently came home with a bag of candy. His mother Laura asks where he got it from, and Liam says a friend gave it to him. Laura does not believe him and lectures him. That he should come home right after school and not hang out. And certainly, don't buy candy. Liam says all his friends do. Laura tells him that she doesn't care. He has to come home. A week later, she catches him with candy again. Her sermon seems to have done nothing.

The Power of Mentalizing. Joost Hutsebaut, Liesbet Nijssens, and Miriam van Vessem, Oxford University Press.
© Joost Hutsebaut, Liesbet Nijssens, Miriam van Vessem 2023. DOI: 10.1093/oso/9780198880677.003.0006

Suppose that people would learn unconditionally from others, Liam would immediately be corrected by Laura. We know it doesn't work that way. Just like it doesn't always help to tell a friend she looks fine if she thinks she's too fat. On the contrary, compliments often slip from people with negative self-esteem. 'You're only saying it because you're my girlfriend. If you were really honest, you would say something different.' In other words: learning does not happen automatically and naturally.

Likewise with Liam. Liam is of an age when the pressure to fit in socially and to fit in with the group increases. Perhaps he still has too little 'I' or individuality to be able to separate himself sufficiently from the group. Especially if Liam is a somewhat insecure boy, with little self-confidence, this increases the chance that he becomes too dependent on the group norms that apply in the group he wants to belong to. In the example, it is especially emphasized that mother's sermon does not impress. It does not lead to behavioural change and does not seem to help Liam enough to distinguish himself from his group of 'friends'. If his group becomes even more destructive or aggressive after school, his dependence may become highly problematic. That is why it is important for Liam's mother to know how to reach him so that she can teach him about the dangers in the world.

> Do you recognize something like this? Have you experienced that other people (your partner, client, child, student, colleague) do not accept something from you, even though you are sincerely convinced that it would be better for him or her? That they ignore your advice, no matter how well you mean it? Do you have an idea why?

Epistemic trust

In order to be able to learn anything from another person, a number of conditions must be met. This chapter deals with one of these conditions: *epistemic trust*. A somewhat complex term that refers to the trust in others that underlies someone's willingness to accept knowledge from others, or: trust in the other person as someone who has something meaningful to teach you.

Epistemic trust rests on two pillars. First, you must be able to rely on the other person's *reliable* knowledge. You can trust a garage owner if you feel that he or she knows a lot about cars. You can trust your therapist if you feel that he or she knows a lot about the symptoms you are dealing with. And you trust your teacher if you have the impression that he or she knows the field well.

But perhaps this is not enough. A second condition is therefore that you have the idea that this knowledge is *personally relevant* to you. If you have the idea that the garage owner does not have your interests in mind, or that your practitioner knows the theory but has no idea who you actually are, then you may not accept the knowledge they offer. And if you feel that your teacher cannot explain to you why you need that knowledge for your job later on, then you may only be studying for your exams. Conversely, if you have the idea that the garage owner really makes an effort to understand your wishes and really wants to take them into account, you will have more confidence in his or her advice. And if you have the idea that your practitioner really understands what is going on inside you, then you are more likely to become curious about his or her approach. Personally relevant to you thus means that you have the idea that the other person sincerely and honestly matches your needs, interests, feelings, and wishes.

> **Epistemic trust** is trusting that the other person has knowledge that is reliable as well as personally relevant or helpful to you. Therefore, you are willing to absorb that knowledge.

What applies to the inclusion of relatively simple skills, such as handling cutlery, also applies to more complex knowledge. For example, when someone tells you something about yourself, and you consider that knowledge to be reliable, personally relevant, and useful, you absorb that knowledge more easily. So, if your parents align themselves well with who you are, and then describe how they appreciate you being caring and helpful, then you accept that knowledge about yourself: I am someone who is caring and helpful. This information becomes part of your self-image: this is who I am. And if your parents really got to know you well as a person and assess your qualities well, then that knowledge about yourself is invaluable in the rest of your life.

> What parts of your self-image have you borrowed from your parents, for example, because they repeatedly emphasized those qualities?

Epistemic vigilance

Your ability to recognize reliable and relevant knowledge therefore influences the quality and effectiveness of the learning process. After all, it is better to ignore unreliable knowledge. Perhaps this is one of the biggest concerns of parents: will my child be able to find friends and adults who can impart accurate, reliable, and useful knowledge? Or will my child get carried away by untrustworthy others? After all, not all knowledge is helpful and reliable. The world is teeming with *fake news*, and this phenomenon is not limited to social media. For example, if you buy a new house, the broker will mainly highlight the strong sides of the house and distract from the lesser sides.

In addition to a basic trust in others, from which we open ourselves to what they can teach us, we also need a healthy dose of vigilance. That vigilance keeps us alert, so that we don't adopt unreliable or harmful information. She ensures that we are not naive. In addition to epistemic trust, we therefore also need *epistemic vigilance* as a counterbalance.

Elijah and Jonas
Fifteen-year-old Elijah regularly goes skating in the park with his friend Jonas. One day Jonas' brother is there too, with a friend. They are a few years older. The friend has brought weed with him. 'You should try it too.' Elijah hesitates, he doesn't feel comfortable with it. 'Come on, don't be such a jerk. One joint can't hurt. How old are you?'

As a parent you would like Elijah to refuse. How reliable is this boy's information? Can one joint do no harm? And a second? As a parent, you would want Elijah not only to have a healthy dose of confidence, but also to be vigilant and not just believe everything from others. So he can say, 'No, I don't want this.'

> How would you help Elijah with this as a parent? Do you have any ideas about how you could help Elijah to rely on 'close' friends? Do you have experience with this in your own life?

However, young people are easily influenced. Take the phenomenon of 'vlogging', for example, keeping a weblog with videos. Its creators, vloggers, exert a lot of influence on their mostly young followers. That's because their audience really feels seen and understood, because the vlogger addresses his or her viewers in a recognizable way. Not only vloggers can do that, politicians are sometimes very good at it too. For example, in 2016 Donald Trump managed to touch a mass of voters with his discourse, unlike Hillary Clinton. Perhaps many Americans did not trust her intentions and took an epistemic vigilance toward her message. These examples illustrate the dangers of rhetoric and charisma. Sometimes people can become *epistemically naive* and uncritically follow the example of others. Then politicians can make statements that are unworldly, dangerous, or simply untrue without their supporters giving up. When it comes to epistemic trust, the content of the message is sometimes subordinate to who is delivering the message.

> **Epistemic vigilance** is the ability to suspend epistemic trust (i.e., to fend off unreliable information that is irrelevant to you). It helps you to distinguish between reliable and less reliable sources of information.

The development of epistemic trust

Children must *learn* to learn from others. Epistemic trust does not come naturally, even though children may seem naive and gullible. We are not naturally open to the 'good' intentions of others. Such a naive attitude towards the outside world could even be very unwise. If you start out believing in the goodness of the environment and that environment turns out to be harmful, then it threatens your chances of survival. To give a simple evolutionary example, if our ancestors had assumed that all animals were harmless or all mushrooms edible, it would have cost them dearly. We are by nature much more alert to the negative than to the positive, so we give more importance to something potentially dangerous or unreliable than to something we consider safe. Another simple example: describe a job applicant to your colleague in ten characteristics, of which eight are positive and two are negative. Chances are that your colleague mainly gives weight to those two negative qualities in his or her assessment. Alertness to negative information, or epistemic vigilance, is much more important for survival than openness to positive information, or epistemic trust. Whether you eat only three of a hundred kinds of edible mushrooms or all hundred, it doesn't make much difference to your survival, as long as you don't eat that one poisonous kind.

Therefore, epistemic trust, or the openness to new information and the willingness to allow it to be absorbed and used, must be developed. No doubt people have some kind of predisposition to develop this—because we have to learn—but that predisposition needs incentives to flourish. The most important stimulus is the experience of security and attunement in a relationship, which we have discussed extensively in the previous chapters. Parents who are well attuned to their child and mirror their child, have a sense of his or her emotions and needs well enough, and ensure safety and relaxation in contact.

It is this basic security that diminishes the natural epistemic vigilance and creates space for epistemic trust. In other words, these parents give their child the confidence that they can temporarily suspend epistemic vigilance, so that they are open to what the parents are teaching him or her.

The learning process may proceed as follows. The child feels that the parent really understands him or her, is really attuned to him or her, and therefore trusts that parent has something to teach him or her. The result of such a sufficiently good development is that the child (and later the adult) dares to trust the other person and his or her knowledge. In addition, it will usually attach more value to the knowledge and advice of people it knows and who are important to him or her, the attachment figures. Nevertheless, the child will suspend this trust if the other person's knowledge proves to be unreliable. 'I trust mum's judgement, unless reality shows that her judgement is really wrong in this particular case. Then I rely more on my own assessment.' Secure attachment therefore leads to trust in the other, as well as to trust in yourself. You dare to be open to the opinions, insights, and advice of the other, but you also have enough self-confidence to form your own opinion when necessary. You dare to make yourself dependent and lean on others, but you also dare to go against the other and follow your own path.

Thomas and Victoria
Thomas is Victoria's biology teacher in the penultimate year of secondary education. His colleagues complain about the atmosphere in Victoria's class. They don't listen, they can't be controlled ... Nothing seems to interest today's youth. Thomas doesn't recognize that. He finds Victoria's class very nice and interested. Victoria also thinks Thomas is her best teacher. He is not difficult and has a good sense of what the class finds interesting. She hangs on his every word. When Thomas encourages the class to demonstrate for the climate, they all make plans. The funny thing is that they probably wouldn't have done that with another teacher.

Have you known a teacher like Thomas yourself? What did that teacher do in order to fascinate you so much that he or she has remained in your memory?

Thomas is one of those teachers we all remember. His lessons transcend his field: they are lessons about and for life. Perhaps the gift of teachers like Thomas is that they are perfectly able to sense and adjust to the temperature in the classroom and the students, but without losing their individuality—they are not out to please the class at whatever it costs. These are often teachers who have a positive attitude towards students, who have an eye for their emotional needs and who stimulate them in their autonomy. This implies that they dare to make real contact with the class and immerse themselves in the atmosphere that prevails there, and neither try to control it nor flee from it. These teachers may understand the meaning of disruptive behaviour and can address it by focusing on that underlying meaning rather than just limiting the behaviour itself.

The example illustrates again why effective mentalizing is so important. Essentially, mentalizing is forming a picture of the needs, feelings, and thoughts of the other person, and helping that other person form a sufficiently accurate picture of your intentions. When you mentalize another person, you are making an effort to really understand the other person from within so that they can experience your knowledge as personally relevant. If your student states that, for example, you only do your work as a teacher for money and not because you are really involved and want the best for him or her, then there is little chance that epistemic trust will be triggered.

Chloe and Nicole
Chloe has her first conversation with her therapist, Nicole. She doesn't like her. Nicole immediately starts to act positive: it's great that she came ('Yes, she had to . . .') and she is wearing very nice pants ('Shut up, old pie'). She quickly feels patronized. Her therapist sprinkles compliments that completely slide off her. For Chloe, it just feels like a therapist trick.

Chloe will not 'learn' much from her therapist in this session. Why not? Not necessarily because the therapist is not an expert, but because Chloe does not experience the therapist's intentions as sincere. She experiences the compliments as irritating. She is full of assumptions about the therapist and her intentions, and as a result she no longer believes her. If you think it's just a trick, then you don't let that fool you, do you? This simple example shows that compliments or reinforcements don't always work. They must be attuned to the mental state of the other. That requires a *relationship* in which you feel that the other person is mentalizing about you, which also allows you to better mentalize about the other person's intentions. If that goes wrong, then something similar might happen as what happened to Chloe.

The extent to which a person is able to connect others to himself, to reach others, differs between individuals. Otherwise, Victoria might not only hang on Thomas' every word, but also on those of other teachers. But what determines whether someone actually opens up to the knowledge of the other?

We would like to illustrate this with the following experiment, in which two objects of indefinite shape are introduced to toddlers. These are 'invented' objects that do not occur in the everyday world and that do not evoke any particular preference or dislike. The examiner introduces these two objects to the child, but shapes that introduction in two different ways so that we can compare their effects. In the first condition, a woman first makes extensive and explicit contact with the child, for example, by making eye contact and calling the child by name. This establishes a relationship. In the second condition, the woman avoids contact and just looks at the table between her and the child. Then, in both conditions, she looks delighted at one object and disgusted at the other. Finally, she asks the child to give her one of the two objects. In a variation on this experiment, the woman sitting with the child does not ask for an object, but another researcher comes in and asks the child for one of the two objects.

What seems to be the case? In the variant in which the woman does not explicitly make contact with the child before asking for an object, the child clearly gives her the 'attractive' object more often. The child has learned that this person has a clear preference for one of the two objects and acts accordingly. However, in this variant, when another researcher comes in at the end and asks for an object, the child does not give one object more often than the other. This could be interpreted as follows: the child has learned that the first woman has a clear preference, but does not extend this knowledge to another person. The knowledge only applies in a specific situation (this woman) and is not generalized. Note, however, that if the woman does connect with the child prior to looking with delight or disgust at the objects, then surprisingly, the child will be more likely to give the attractive object to the unfamiliar researcher as well. Making contact therefore has something to do with the way in which the knowledge is absorbed. In this example, the child hasn't learned that a particular woman finds a particular object more attractive, but that the particular object is more attractive in general, also to other persons. The knowledge is generalized from situational (valid in the here-and-now) to general knowledge (valid all the time). To put it a bit dramatically: the child has learned 'for life', and not just for this situation.

This experiment teaches us about the importance of making connection for activating epistemic trust. Making contact is necessary if you want people to open up to what you have to teach them. A therapist with whom you 'click' may be someone who succeeds in making real contact with the client.

> What does a 'click' mean to you? Have you had mentors, teachers, practitioners, or friends with whom you really clicked? What was it that caused the click?

Grasping attention

When someone else succeeds in making a real connection with you, you often become curious about how that other person looks at the world, at others, and at you. Such fruitful contact is especially created when you feel that the other person is mentalizing you well, when you feel that the other person really pays attention to you *as a person*. If you feel recognized and acknowledged in the contact, it reduces your tendency to be suspicious, and you feel trust in the other person. This is the basis on which you become open to what the other person has to teach you.

Barry and Mehar
Barry is 44 years old. He drinks too much. Daniella, his partner, has already addressed his drinking numerous times. She thinks he should be treated for his alcohol problem. He thinks she's whining. Precisely by nagging at him like that, she makes him even more tense, which only makes him drink more. Barry's mother has also spoke to him about his drinking problem. Barry feels bad about it, but often reacts irritated. He doesn't want anyone to interfere with his drinking, but on the other hand, he is also a bit concerned about his drinking.

He finally decided to talk to his GP, Mehar. Surprisingly, she doesn't immediately start listing all kinds of health advice. Instead, she says she assumes that Barry himself knows that he needs to drink less, otherwise he wouldn't have come, but that perhaps he wants to make it clear that he can't do it alone. And she asks him what it is like for him when he doesn't drink or drinks less. Barry tells her how terribly bad he feels. Also, because Daniella thinks it's normal not to drink and doesn't seem to see how much effort it takes and how terrible he feels. His doctor's compassionate and supportive response gives Barry the feeling that for the first time someone else can understand the burden he is experiencing. But at the same time, Mehar defends his partner: she must suffer a lot from the consequences of Barry's drinking. He'd been on the defensive when his mother almost literally said the same thing to him. Strangely enough, now he accepts that comment. At the end of the conversation, Mehar concludes: 'Barry, I think I understand a little more how stuck you feel. You do want to drink less, but every time you try to stop, you feel terribly bad. Daniella and your mother are concerned, but their approach is not helping you. On the contrary, it seems to be making you even more alone. So, my advice would be to seek the help of someone who is not so close to you, such as a therapist.' For the first time, Barry is open to such advice.

Barry's GP managed to make contact. Mehar has thought about Barry and the position he must be in. She made him feel that she understood something of what it must be like to be Barry. Due to this connection, the advice that Barry had received countless times before, could now land. Of course, it's a lot easier for the GP to keep mentalizing about Barry: she is a little further away from the problems and less affected by them. Both Daniella and Barry's mother may not have enough mental space to properly mentalize Barry to make the connection necessary to reach him with their advice.

In addition, another important thing emerges in this example. When Mehar senses there is an opening, she calls Barry by name. We call this signal an *ostensive cue*, or in other words: a communication signal. Ostensive cues communicate that something important is coming. You grab the attention: 'Now I'm going to teach you something.' In fact, Mehar does something that parents often do with their child. When parents want to teach their child something, they tune in to him or her, and the moment an important message follows, they try to attract attention. They create a click, as it were, in a very natural way, a moment when something can be learned. They call their child by name, or say something like, 'Pay attention!' or, 'Now listen carefully!' In a relationship where there is real contact, communication signals activate epistemic trust (or deactivate epistemic vigilance: 'It is now safe to learn'). In this way they create the context in which learning can take place. The other person realizes: 'Now it becomes important, I have to remember what the other person tells me.' The advice can enter the person's mind: it matches someone's feelings and needs, and is therefore received as personally relevant knowledge.

Good speakers often make use of a whole arsenal of ostensive cues, just like sensitive parents who want to teach their child something: they have their audience in mind, they address the listener almost personally, accentuate their message with strategic gestures: 'Read my lips!'

How do you create a fertile foundation for social learning?
1. Make a real connection by mentalizing the other person.
2. This decreases epistemic vigilance and activates epistemic trust.
3. Use ostensive cues (speech, eye contact, name-calling, etc.): 'Note, what I'm about to say is important.'

4. This signal ensures that the other person is alert to what you are about to say.
5. The recipient is open to receiving knowledge that is important on a personal and social level.
6. Here, the recipient learns something that is also important in other situations.

Summary

Better learning is achieved when we strike a balance between epistemic trust and epistemic vigilance. In normal development, this is achieved thanks to the security we experience in contact, and thanks to parents who mentalize about us and help us mentalize about ourselves and others. The latter is necessary to separate good from less good intentions, to admit the right knowledge and to exclude unreliable knowledge.

In the vulnerable triangle of mentalizing, attachment, and social learning, different forms of insecurity that children experience in their basic relationships can influence the development of epistemic trust. We will discuss these consequences in the next chapter.

7

Epistemic mistrust, naivety, and hypervigilance

In a healthy environment, parents are sufficiently attuned to their child. They effectively mentalize about him or her, ensuring safety in contact, instilling the epistemic trust that helps a child learn from them and acquire knowledge and skills that will help them function better as an independent adult. Good mentalizing, secure attachment, and epistemic trust go hand in hand. But what happens to the development of this epistemic trust when a child does not grow up in such a safe, attuned, effectively mentalizing environment? What if, for whatever reason, caregivers are less attuned to their child?

> Do you remember Sophia from Chapter 5 on insecure attachment? Can she safely learn from Patty? What effect would this have on her openness to learn from others later in life? What if Sophia is later called in to talk to her mentor or care teacher? What if the school psychologist is concerned? What if she comes into treatment? How safe is it for Sophia to open up to others?

In an environment that is less safe, there are roughly three options. The first is to cut yourself off completely from that environment and not adopt anything more from it. The environment is harmful and unreliable, and you no longer dare to lean on another person, only on yourself. We call this *epistemic mistrust*. The second option is to nevertheless look for an anchor to cling to in that unsafe environment. The environment is harmful, and you are hyper-alert to possible unreliability (*epistemic hypervigilance*), while at the same time you are clinging anxiously to what in reality may be little more than a straw, on which you rely almost uncritically (*epistemic naivety*). In addition, there is a third option, namely that you do not dare to trust yourself or anyone else, and thus become completely isolated. You are then caught in an epistemic dilemma.

The Power of Mentalizing. Joost Hutsebaut, Liesbet Nijssens, and Miriam van Vessem, Oxford University Press.
© Joost Hutsebaut, Liesbet Nijssens, Miriam van Vessem 2023. DOI: 10.1093/oso/9780198880677.003.0007

Healthy development requires a balance of epistemic trust and epistemic vigilance. In less favourable developments, epistemic distrust, epistemic hypervigilance, or epistemic naivety predominate.

Epistemic mistrust

Sometimes your experiences can lead you to look at the other person with suspicion. Then it becomes difficult to open up to what the other person could teach you.

> *Daniel*
> *Daniel's father used to be an alcoholic. Daniel was very ashamed of that. He thought his mother was too soft to go against his father and his problems. Early on, Daniel started to withdraw. He took very little involvement from his parents. He also isolated himself at school. He doesn't want them to find out how bad his home situation is. He doesn't have much of a need for others. He paddles his own canoe. In the end, you can only rely on yourself in life.*

Daniel no longer learns, or at least no longer learns from others. He shuts himself off. Daniel has created *epistemic mistrust* in others. He can only rely on himself. Solutions that he comes up with himself are good. What comes from the outside cannot get a hold of him.

> Epistemic mistrust means that new knowledge is considered unreliable or irrelevant, and therefore kept out: 'I don't trust anyone but myself.'

Epistemic hypervigilance and naivety

Your experiences can also lead to you being very alert to possibly unreliable knowledge of others (hypervigilance), but at the same time being so insecure and anxious that you cling blindly to one person. Such dependence can sometimes go way too far (extreme examples are lover-boy relationships).

> *Chelsea*
> *Learning doesn't come naturally to Chelsea. She seems to have become immune to people who mean her well, and positive experiences or feedback seem to slide*

off her. When Chelsea's mom says she's proud of her, Chelsea can't believe it. Chelsea is stuck with herself. She feels lonely and misunderstood. There's no one she's really friends with and her parents don't seem to realize how terribly bad she feels. She often seeks support on forums, where girls her age exchange messages. Recently, one of those girls advised her to scratch herself. 'That will give you relief,' she wrote. Chelsea tried it and since then she self-harms almost daily.

Chelsea is unreachable for positive experiences and feedback. Perhaps they are even feeding her sense of being misunderstood. She may be full of epistemic hypervigilance. At the same time, however, she yearns for someone who does understand her, a kind of epistemic hunger. She therefore seeks refuge elsewhere, outside the family, and is open to 'unreliable' sources of information. Perhaps this also explains why young people with problems look for each other so often: they recognize each other. This epistemic hunger can become a breeding ground for *epistemic naivety*: accepting uncritically what the other person who understands you tells you. Perhaps this is one of the mechanisms behind the spread of problems among young people. If someone you trust and identify with solves his or her problems in a certain—destructive—way, it may be tempting to start applying those solutions yourself.

Epistemic hypervigilance refers to excessive alertness and vigilance about the reliability of the knowledge of others, often out of doubt about their intentions: 'You have to be very careful in life!'

Epistemic naivety manifests itself in blind faith in the knowledge of a particular other, and that knowledge is accepted uncritically: 'I trust only you and no one else. Not even myself.'

Epistemic dilemma

Daniel only dares to have trust in himself. He may rely too little on others, so that he can only fall back on his own solutions and convictions, but at least he still finds some support in himself. Chelsea, in turn, finds very little support in herself, but desperately searches for others to cling to. Maybe not healthy, but at least it gives her some support when she doesn't know what to do anymore. But what if you do not find anything to hold on to, neither within yourself nor outside of yourself?

Gabriella
It's night. Gabriella lies awake. She is anxious and cannot stop the stream of
thoughts in her head. She wishes she had someone with her to reassure her.
She hesitates in front of her mother's room but goes back to her own room an-
yway. She cannot go to her mother. She is depressed and often takes sleeping
pills. She is also afraid of her reaction. Sometimes she is understanding, but at
other times she can get really angry when Gabriella needs her. There is no one
who can help her anyway. Or maybe on one of the fora she often visits? She then
starts chatting with strange men. It doesn't help, but she feels seen for a mo-
ment. And then dirty again.

Gabriella is stuck in an *epistemic dilemma*: she craves to trust others, and she
needs others, but at the same time she fears that the other person will harm
her. In short, Gabriella has no firm ground beneath her feet. She doesn't know
who or what to trust. She has no anchor point, neither within herself nor outside herself.

> Do you recognize people in your environment who function in one of these styles? For
> example, people who you notice don't accept much from you? Or a friend who fully
> trusts that one man or woman you hoped he or she would ignore? Why is that, you
> think? What is the effect of that on you?

Attachment styles and epistemic trust

Openness to learn from others must be acquired. In the examples above, that
openness has been damaged. This leads to several problems in social learning.
Gabriella, Chelsea, and Daniel have too little balance between epistemic trust
and epistemic vigilance. But how did this come about?

> Can you imagine which of these epistemic strategies might correspond to the dif-
> ferent attachment styles?

Research shows that the predisposition or tendency towards epistemic
trust, mistrust, or naivety is related to the type of attachment style a child
develops. There is a very nice study that has examined this in children.
In the experiment, three- to four-year-olds are shown strange hybrid

animals, for example an animal that is half fish and half bird. Usually, 50 per cent is one animal and 50 per cent another, but sometimes the proportion is changed so that the picture represents 75 per cent one animal and only 25 per cent the other, for example just the fins of the fish on the back of a bird. The children are asked which animal they see. Before they can express their own opinion, they are first given the opinion of both mother (the main attachment figure) and a stranger. Now the test is designed in such a way that the stranger always gives the other option. If mother says the hybrid animal is a fish, the stranger says a bird, and vice versa. With the 75/25 animals, the mother always refers to the 'minority animal'. The question now is what the child will do: Will he or she follow his or her mother or the stranger? Interestingly, the child's choice appears to be related to attachment style.

Securely attached children tend to follow their mother's opinion. If the drawing, which represents 'reality', does not provide a definitive answer—in the case of the 50/50 animals—then securely attached children clearly more often follow the choice that mother makes than that of the stranger. However, when the drawing clearly points in one direction—in the 75/25 animals—then the strategy of securely attached children changes. They then no longer follow the 'unreliable' information of mother and follow the stranger (or perhaps better: trust their own judgement). Securely attached children thus show—as might be expected—a combination of epistemic trust and epistemic vigilance: they basically trust the people with whom they feel securely attached, unless they are evidently wrong. Then they rely on themselves.

Avoidantly attached children (think of Daniel) show a different reaction pattern. Not surprisingly, in the 75/25 animals, they mostly follow the stranger. Remarkably, however, in the 50/50 animals they follow mother as often as the stranger. That's interesting: they don't rely more on the opinion of an attachment figure than on that of a stranger. Or perhaps more correctly: they rely only on their own judgement. They are not influenced by the other. This may be a reflection of their epistemic distrust.

Anxious-ambivalently attached children (think of Chelsea) show yet another pattern. With the 50/50 animals they follow mother in almost all cases. Where reality doesn't really steer them in one direction, they trust their attachment figure almost exclusively. Possibly even more remarkable: also in the 75/25 animals they follow their mother more often than the stranger. This is interesting: even though the reality screams that mother is wrong, yet anxiously ambivalently attached children continue to follow their attachment figure. This can be interpreted as epistemic naivety. This goes hand in hand with very little trust in strangers. Even though the stranger is clearly right, the child mistrusts his or her opinion: epistemic hypervigilance.

Finally, there are the *disorganized* attached children (think of Gabriella), who are often traumatized and have experienced that the people they depend on can also harm them. An intriguing pattern of reaction is also found in these children: whether 50/50 animals or 75/25 animals, they follow their mother as often as the stranger. In fact, they seem to answer almost randomly: reality has no influence on their answers, any more than the relationship with the other person. These children seem to trust neither the other nor themselves. Their random answers may reflect something of their epistemic dilemma.

The basic attachment style that a person has developed in his or her life thus seems to be able to predict how and from whom people learn. If you are *securely* attached, you develop a basic predisposition to learn from others, but at the same time you critically examine whether what the other person wants to teach you is reliable. This is an incredibly valuable asset. You ultimately learn not only from your parents, but also from other people based on this predisposition. You will be able to further refine your own insights, your image of yourself and of the world, in order to adapt better and better to the world around you. If you are securely attached and have a basic attitude of epistemic trust, it is usually easier to create relationships in which you can learn. You are also usually quite flexible and not so stuck in your own truth, so you can more easily accept that there are other visions besides your own view of things. At the same time, you continue to think autonomously and critically whether new information is correct, and you will not just accept unreliable information.

On the other hand, if someone is *avoidantly* attached, the basic attitude is aimed at warding off the knowledge of others. Perhaps these people have experienced more often that others do not adequately attune themselves to them and this is why they have closed themselves off from the outside world. They may want to trust the other person, but that feels too scary and unsafe, so they rely only on themselves. Avoidantly attached individuals are often much harder to reach. They carry a thick armour, are too autonomous. So, these are people who do not readily accept help from others. 'In the end you are on your own in life' seems to be their motto. They are also not likely to seek help, and if they do, they are often sceptical and suspicious. They don't make connection and don't just open up to advice. That often makes them rigid. What they experience and think is correct. It is often hard work for those around them to break through the armour of epistemic distrust. To this end, the other person must first of all invest strongly in establishing affective contact. With avoidant attachment people, it is often not just a matter of persevering, but the other person also has to really 'squeeze' into the contact in order to touch the avoidant person and trigger his or her interest.

If someone has an *anxious-ambivalent* attachment, they are often very picky when it comes to putting trust in others, but once they trust someone else, the trust is blind. Blind to the extent that these persons hardly think autonomously and critically and rely uncritically on what that one person tells them. They often make black and white choices: it clicks with that teacher, but not with the other three. And when it clicks, they no longer reflect on what they think and want, and they let themselves be led by the other person. Think of the woman who consults her partner with every choice or the adolescent who does everything for the approval of his gymnastics coach. The point is that they don't develop confidence in their own capacity to make choices or to deal with the fear they experience. They remain dependent on the other. If this anchor point (i.e., the partner, the coach, the therapist, etc.) disappears from their view, then it is likely that they will either place their insecurity or fear with someone else or that their problems will come back in full force. Their 'self' is too fragile. The only thing that really helps to break the circle in this situation is the experience that you have your own opinion, can make your own choices and handle fearful situations yourself; in short, you develop self-confidence.

Finally, when a person is *disorganized* attached, he or she often has no clear epistemic strategy. They dare neither to trust themselves nor the other. Information is not judged well, so these people are often unpredictable, that is, in who they follow or in what their opinion is on a certain topic. They often feel very insecure, anxious, and unstable. They experience little ground beneath their feet. They want to trust others, but this is too unsafe and unpredictable. Others have to invest a lot and have a lot of patience to create something of security in the relationship. Only then, something of epistemic trust—and thus new and healthier learning—can arise.

The different epistemic strategies, depending on someone's attachment style, are summarized in Table 7.1.

You can imagine that each of these learning styles or epistemic strategies also influences your contact with others. With epistemic mistrusting people you bump into a wall of mistrust. Whatever you hand them, it seems to slide off them. That can cause a lot of frustration. With epistemic hypervigilant people you have to prove your good intentions again and again. They seem to want to believe that what you say is true and has value, but they don't dare to believe you. Finally, with epistemic naive people it can sometimes feel oppressive that they lean on you like that. You are made too important and you wish they could lean on others too. Or on their own.

Table 7.1 Attachment styles and associated epistemic strategies

Attachment style	Epistemic strategy
Secure attachment	Epistemic trust *I can rely enough on my own opinion/experience.* *I trust the opinion/experience of others, especially attachment* *figures, if it is sufficiently credible.*
Avoidant attachment	Epistemic mistrust *I can only rely on myself.*
Anxious-ambivalent attachment	Epistemic hypervigilance *I don't trust my own opinion/experience.* Epistemic naivety *If I really trust someone, then my trust is blind.*
Disorganized attachment	Epistemic dilemma *I don't trust myself and therefore need confirmation from others,* *but . . .* *I don't trust others and so have to rely on myself, but . . .*

Connecting with epistemic vulnerable people

Epistemic hypervigilance and epistemic distrust mean that there is no more learning from others. Epistemic naivety makes someone very selective in dealing with knowledge from others. But what is the consequence?

Chloe is convinced that she is a nuisance, is ugly, can't do anything. What worth does she have for her parents? When something bad happens, this only confirms her negative image of herself. Her mother sometimes complains that Chloe doesn't consider all the positive things she does are worthwhile. She's certainly not ugly, says mother, and she's certainly not the only one who thinks that! On the contrary, she's a very pretty girl. It doesn't impress Chloe.

> Do you know any Chloes in your environment? What makes your Chloe so hard to deal with? How does that affect you?

This is Chloe who, in Chapter 6, was turned off by the compliments during the introductory meeting with her therapist. She doesn't believe anything from others and certainly nothing that deviates from what she already 'knows' about herself, which is that she is ugly and worthless. Chloe's epistemic hypervigilance keeps her from letting in others' opinions about herself. Either they don't mean it or she wants to believe them but she doesn't dare. The result is that nothing changes in Chloe's self-image. She stubbornly clings to rigid, entrenched beliefs about herself.

People with mental health problems often cling remarkably tightly to ways of thinking, feeling, and acting that are not helpful, even though others have made it clear countless times that this is not correct. They don't take those well-intentioned warnings and cling to the truth in their minds as they know it. *Rigidity* is pretty much the key feature behind mental health problems. Rigidity is opposed to flexibility. Flexibility means you can easily adapt; that in order to progress, you can adopt other ways of thinking and acting and not persist in ineffective strategies. Flexibility requires epistemic trust. And vice versa, rigidity and epistemic mistrust and epistemic hypervigilance also go hand in hand. We will come back to this in more detail in Chapter 10. We discuss how rigidity and lack of epistemic trust often make someone vulnerable to developing psychological problems.

Before concluding this chapter, let us briefly relate it to the previous chapter. There, we described the conditions under which epistemic trust can be activated. We emphasized that making 'real' contact, using ostensive cues (communication signals), mentalizing and feeling mentalized determine the extent to which someone opens up to the knowledge of the other in a relationship. But does this also work when there is epistemic distrust or epistemic hypervigilance? Is there a way to reach epistemic mistrusting individuals?

Alexandra and Anna
Anna is Alexandra's English teacher. She is not her mentor, but she always likes to have her in the classroom. Alexandra writes beautiful poems. At the same time, Anna noticed that those poems have a somewhat dark edge, and she has had an eye out for her ever since. When Alexandra handed in her homework recently, Anna noticed some symmetrical scratches on her wrist. That made her suspect that something was definitely wrong. She had noticed for a while that Alexandra was more on her own in class. She was also quieter than last year.

When Alexandra leaves the classroom that day, Anna addresses her briefly: 'Hi Alexandra, do you want to stay just a little longer? I want to talk to you.' Anna tells Alexandra as honestly and directly as possible that she has been worried for a while and that she had just noticed that she has small scars on her wrist. Alexandra lowers her eyes and doesn't respond. Anna tries to attune to Alexandra's mental state: 'I can imagine that I am scaring you and maybe you don't like it that I talk to you about this. I'm talking about it because I'm concerned about you and I think it's important that you know that. I want you to know that you can always talk to me if you want to.'

> *Alexandra is a bit confused. Of course, she is ashamed, but on the other hand it is also nice that Anna has noticed that things are not going well. And that she gives her the space to decide for herself if and when she wants to come back to it. It helps her, if she can think about what she wants to say in a conversation.*

Again, in this example, effective mentalizing is the key word, or the key … Anna reflects on Alexandra's mind. About what could be going on and how Alexandra might feel, but also about what it is like for her to be approached by a teacher who is concerned about her. Anna tries to keep in touch with Alexandra's emotions when she speaks to her. This creates a safe environment in which real contact can be established and Anna can create emotional closeness. But she also gives space to Alexandra: 'You can always address me if you want to.'

> Now that you have read this chapter, can you consider whether you have encountered such a complex attitude with someone close to you? Can you relate this to any of these epistemic styles? Can you think of what might have helped in that situation? What had to be understood? What could you have mentalized about?

Summary

In this chapter, we described how poor development of epistemic trust goes hand in hand with the experience of insecurity in basic relationships and with disruptions in the development of mentalizing. Avoidantly attached individuals will often close themselves off: epistemic mistrust. Possibly this distrust was functional in childhood, because the environment was harmful, but as a growing adolescent and as an adult, it is often no longer functional to hold on to it. Anxious-ambivalently attached individuals often rely too heavily on one attachment figure and have developed too little 'self', too little autonomy, to suspend that trust when necessary. That makes them vulnerable to entanglement in dependent relationships. They are epistemically hypervigilant towards almost everyone, but epistemically naive towards that one attachment figure who knows how to reach them. Disorganized attached individuals are often deeply confused and isolated. They dare not trust themselves or others. These learning dispositions influence the contact they have with others. Often such people come across as quite rigid and closed, while securely attached people, with a healthy dose of epistemic trust and epistemic vigilance, are flexible in their thoughts and actions, and open to the other.

In the next chapter, we'll discuss how to approach and connect with the other person, integrating all of the knowledge from the previous chapters on attachment, mentalizing, and epistemic trust.

8

Tips and tricks to restore effective mentalizing

By restoring your own and other's mentalizing in difficult situations, you can create safety and evoke epistemic trust. Mentalizing is the foundation of good, supportive relationships. It enables us to understand and reach out to each other better. Mentalizing creates a connection. Conversely, non-mentalizing leads to frustration, misunderstanding, friction, and sometimes loneliness. In the previous chapters we gave numerous examples of how mentalizing sometimes worked better and sometimes less well. Each of these examples showed how great the influence is on the type of contact and interaction that is established. No doubt you recognized some examples in your own life. Perhaps you thought back to moments when you felt a real connection with your partner, a friend, a colleague, your child ... And perhaps you sometimes thought back to moments when it did not work so well. Moments when you were on a completely different wavelength than a colleague, perhaps because you were annoyed by him or her. Or moments when you got into escalating arguments or just ended up in a state of silence with your partner. Moments when you didn't reach your son or daughter, or moments when a client got under your skin. In short, moments when you were not the best version of yourself, when you were not the parent, partner, colleague, or caregiver that you actually want to be.

> Before you read on, take a moment to think about how reading this book has made you reflect upon yourself. Has it affected the way you look at yourself and others? At situations in the team you are part of? At your children? Your relationships?

It is nice to be mentalized, but you may regularly fail to do so adequately. In this chapter, we give some tips on how to restore your own mentalizing and that of others. Unfortunately, these tips are not a ready-made recipe for

The Power of Mentalizing. Joost Hutsebaut, Liesbet Nijssens, and Miriam van Vessem, Oxford University Press.
© Joost Hutsebaut, Liesbet Nijssens, Miriam van Vessem 2023. DOI: 10.1093/oso/9780198880677.003.0008

mentalizing well all the time. Mentalizing is a process of searching, tuning in and trying to understand, and sometimes succeeding, sometimes not. And yet searching again.

Tip 1: Notice when you or someone else is not mentalizing well

Recovering effective mentalizing starts with recognizing a possible loss of it. We have given countless examples of this in the previous chapters. A psychic equivalent mode can be recognized by absolute statements, black-and-white thinking, escalating tension, excessive blaming, suspicion, and filling in thoughts beyond reason. A teleological mode can be recognized by the compelling need for physical action, when one feels compelled to do something, and a pretend mode by emptiness in oneself, boredom in contact, overly rational or cognitive analysis, and aimless brooding. Deficits in mentalizing manifest in various ways. Sometimes the resulting behaviour can be so pleasant that we easily overlook the deficits. Look at the following example:

Prisha and Jonas
The atmosphere in the kindergarten is restless. Sarah has got her little fingers caught in the door and is crying badly. The teacher takes care of Sarah: she goes to get a cold pack and tries to comfort her. Some chaos ensues. Jonas climbs onto a bench and jumps off noisily. Some other kids follow. Then he starts an imaginary sword fight. Prisha quietly stands next to the teacher and caresses Sarah's head a few times. When Sarah has stopped crying, she puts her arm around her and says: 'Come with me, I'll stay with you, we can play quietly together'. Then she pulls a funny face, which makes Sarah smile again.

> Consider this example. How do you interpret Jonas' and Prisha's reactions to the uproar that has been caused?

Let's admit: for the order in the classroom, Prisha's behaviour is much nicer than Jonas' fussiness. If we focus only on the behaviour of both, it is tempting to call Prisha 'well behaved' and Jonas 'naughty'. 'Take Prisha as an example, Jonas, she is very good at helping the teacher!'

And yet ... although the behaviour differs, it is reasonable to assume that both Jonas and Prisha are startled by Sarah's shouting and the sudden commotion in the classroom. Only they handle that fright differently. They have different strategies for dealing with their own emotions in such an arousing situation. Jonas becomes anxious and rebellious, and Prisha very caring. Jonas reacts to his tension without paying much attention to the impact of his behaviour on the other children and the teacher. Due to his fright, he can no longer effectively mentalize or regulate his own behaviour. From the same startled reaction, Prisha takes extra care of others. Possibly that is her strategy to keep a grip on her own emotions. By fully focusing on caring for Sarah she may get detached from her own fear. She takes care of others and stops thinking about what she feels and what she needs.

If the teacher does not pay attention to the reduced mentalizing of both children—which of course easily happens in such a stressful situation—but focuses instead solely on their behaviour, she may be tempted to limit and even punish Jonas, while Prisha may get praise and appreciation for being so brave. In both cases, there is no congruent mirroring. Jonas may be receiving anger, whereas his underlying experience may be something of fear or fright. Prisha may be easily overlooked because she does not pose problems, and her underlying experience may not be acknowledged either.

Of course, we can't really blame the teacher, and it doesn't have to be such a bad thing if something like this happens occasionally. But what if the teacher, in many different situations, only pays attention to behaviour? How likely is it that Jonas will constantly be restricted and punished? And that Prisha's emotions will always be forgotten because she is so quiet and strong?

> What would be the effect on Jonas's and Prisha's self-image if their behaviour was seen as the most important thing instead of their mental state? What would be the effect on the way they deal with their feelings?

Of course, adults also regularly show distortions in their mentalizing, and the consequences sometimes seem positive. For example, let us give the story of Jonathan and Kathleen from Chapter 1 a slightly different twist.

Jonathan and Kathleen
Jonathan and Kathleen have been together for twelve years. Last year, Jonathan had an affair with a colleague at work. Jonathan and Kathleen got through it well together. In fact, Kathleen didn't take it too hard. Something like

that can happen when you've been together for so long. It happens to the best couples. I know Jonathan loves me and I love him. An incident like this doesn't have to jeopardize your relationship. On the contrary, it is an opportunity to strengthen your relationship. Jonathan loves me and I love him, and that's what counts.

It could be that this reaction reflects Kathleen's firm belief in the strength of their relationship. However, it could also be that she is not really connecting with what this incident has meant to her (pretend mode). Is her 'positive' reaction adequate? If Kathleen wants to restore her own mentalizing—in her case, to reconnect with her own feelings—she will first have to recognize that her soothing reaction is hiding or suppressing something of the emotions she is experiencing from the incident.

Tip 2: Restore your own mentalizing

Effective mentalizing is contagious. Unfortunately, so is ineffective mentalizing. If you want to restore the mentalizing of others, your own mentalizing must be sufficiently intact. If you are too tense, irritated, worried, afraid, or angry, you are not likely to succeed in a helpful, mentalizing interaction.

Kevin and Angela
Kevin is sixteen and was allowed to go to a nightclub for the first time tonight. He was supposed to come home at two o'clock, but at half past two he has not arrived yet. His mother Angela is panicking more and more. She is worried, irritated, and angry. David, Kevin's father, has already gone to sleep. When her son arrives at a quarter to three, Angela is very upset: 'How can you do this to me? Why do you frighten me like this? What the hell is going on in that mind of yours?' Kevin rolls his eyes: 'Calm down! I had a flat tyre, and my phone was dead!'

In this situation, Angela is unlikely to have a productive conversation with Kevin in which he understands the effect of his behaviour on her. At the time, she is probably too upset, which reinforces Kevin's lack of mentalizing. And it seems that Kevin becomes somewhat laconic when he no longer mentalizes properly.

When we no longer mentalize well, we often do things that are not helpful. Jonas's teacher might shout through the class that he must go to his place immediately, and her shouting would only increase Jonas's anxiety. A general practitioner will make a referral for another physical examination, even though he or she is sure that nothing will come of it. A counsellor will avoid certain topics out of fear for the client's reaction. A man makes, for the umpteenth time, an unpleasant comment about a habit of his partner, even though he knows that he or she will only react defensively. During a meeting, someone repeatedly tries to convince colleagues that he or she is right, without considering other perspectives. A social worker tells a client how he or she 'actually' feels.

Do you recognize moments when you are or were less able to mentalize? How do you notice this in yourself? At such moments, do you withdraw or do you go into your head? Do you tend to react from your emotions or lash out?

There are several ways to restore your own mentalizing. You can reduce the arousal by stepping out of the situation, counting to ten, or finding distractions otherwise. Angela could have said that she is relieved that Kevin is home safely, but that she is not happy that he did not keep his curfew and that she wants to talk to him about it the next day. This way, she avoids getting caught up in a conversation guided by her anxiety and irritation, in which Kevin is not able to consider her needs after all. Another way of dealing with such complex emotions is to seek out someone—your partner, a friend, a colleague—and vent to them. Another option is to consciously reflect on yourself and slow down your own thinking, to avoid jumping to conclusions. Here is a small example:

> *Kate and Maira*
> *Kate has bought new trousers. She is a bit unsure whether they make her look fat. She takes a picture of herself and texts it to her friend Maira: 'Do these trousers make me look fat?' Less than five seconds later she gets a reply: 'Yes, they do, you have an incredibly fat bottom in those trousers!' Kate swallows. She is startled by Maira's rude reaction. Then she thinks for a moment. She doesn't know Maira like this. She is not one to make fun of her that easily. On the contrary! She texts back: 'Are you kidding me?' 'Sure, what did you think? Awesome trousers!'*

Because of Maira's ambiguous reaction, Kate briefly lapses into ineffective mentalizing. She quickly recovers by asking herself: 'Is this normal behaviour for Maira? If not, she may be teasing me.'

Recovering your own mentalizing is often easier when you feel too much, as in Angela's example. It is more difficult when you feel too little. For Kathleen, it is more important to reconnect with the emotional meaning of Jonathan's cheating than to reduce her own tension. Perhaps she needs to increase her tension by allowing her feelings about the incident to surface. She could, for example, talk about it with a friend. This way, she can put into words what has happened to her and what it means to her.

Tip 3: Mentalize out loud

Good mentalizing, as has been said many times, is contagious. If you have recovered your mentalizing, it is more likely that the other person can also mentalize more effectively. In this regard, it is very helpful to mentalize out loud: you are then verbally explicit about your own inner world.

Iris and Imogen
Iris is a social worker. She has been visiting Imogen at home for several months and finds it frustrating that the process is so slow. She sees that Imogen is neglecting herself and her children. Time and again, Iris tries to create order out of the chaos and put Imogen on the right track, but a few days later nothing is left of her efforts. Iris has secretly given up hope a little, but she tries not to let it show. 'Professionally', she hides her powerlessness and irritation until she realizes that she is not able to help Imogen in this way. Iris realizes that she has started to see Imogen as a 'hopeless case' and that this does not help her or Imogen. Therefore, she talks things through with a colleague to get a better idea of what exactly is going on in relation to Imogen. Based on that conversation, she decides to be open with Imogen:

'Imogen, when I left here last time, I noticed I felt somewhat powerless. I really want to help you and during the home visits I have the idea that it is working, but it seems so difficult to keep on track. I would really like to understand what happens between the home visits and what makes it so difficult for you. At the moment, we don't seem to be achieving the change we both want so badly. I notice that this frustrates me, but maybe it frustrates you too? I also know that this is not how you want things to be...'

If Iris approaches Imogen in this way, there is a good chance that will get Imogen to think about things. Of course, it is important not to give such a message in a blaming or irritated manner, because then Imogen might feel attacked. When Iris has recovered mentalizing about herself sufficiently and is attuned to Imogen's inner world, she can use what she notices in herself (powerlessness) to start a conversation. Chances are that Imogen also feels powerless and that it is precisely this feeling that prevents her from remaining active between Iris's visits.

In the example of Kevin and Angela in the previous tip, Angela could start the conversation she has announced by saying how worried and frightened she was and how she cannot understand why Kevin had not let her know that he would be late. That she didn't know him like that either and had therefore panicked even more. And Kathleen could start the conversation with Jonathan or a friend by expressing her surprise that the whole incident seemed to affect her so little.

> What would it be like for you to be open about your own inner world in contact with another person? Does it feel vulnerable? Or comfortable?

You can explicitly mentalize about your own inner world, but also about that of another person. In the following example, let us assume that Iris has not yet had the conversation described earlier with Imogen.

> *Iris and Imogen have an appointment, but Imogen does not open the door. Iris, however, knows that she is at home and waits patiently. Imogen then calls out through the window: 'Go away, I don't need your bullshit!' Iris consults with a colleague about what to do and decides to send Imogen a text message in which she describes some hypotheses why she thinks Imogen might reject her.*
>
> *'Imogen, I came by a few times and then you let me know you don't need home visits anymore. I don't know why you don't want to see me. Maybe I did something in our last interactions that you found annoying. When I think about myself, I remember feeling a bit powerless during the last visit. Could it be that you noticed that in me and that plays a role? Maybe there are other reasons as well why you don't feel the need to talk to me. Still, I would like to have contact with you again. I hope that you will take some time to respond to this. Greetings, Iris.'*

Iris takes Imogen 'in mind': she tries to look beyond Imogen's behaviour and presents her ideas about the situation, whatever they may be, in order to make Imogen think about the motives behind her behaviour. After all, there is a chance that Imogen herself has little insight into this and only feels that she does not like Iris.

Tip 4: Limit ineffective mentalizing in an empathic way

Sometimes you can only recover your own mentalizing and that of others when the behaviour that is an expression of it stops. As long as Jonas is jumping around, it is difficult for the teacher to reach him and get him to start mentalizing again. Another example:

Viraj, Finley, and Callum
Viraj is a woodwork teacher in special education. Things are sometimes tough. He cannot be everywhere at once, and so things sometimes get out of hand be-fore he even notices. Today Finley and Callum were having a fight. They called each other the most disgusting names. Viraj knows that at times like that it is imperative to act firmly and set limits. He says loud and clear: 'Finley and Callum, you are going to break it up now. I have no idea what has angered you, but I demand that you both stop and calm down. Callum, you sit there with Bert. Finley, you sit on that chair. The rest of you go on with your work. In the last fifteen minutes we're all going to discuss what was going on here.'

We are aware that such an intervention does not always have the desired effect and that much will depend on the bond that Viraj has built up with both boys and with the class. What we mean is that good mentalizing does not mean that you have to let all behaviour pass. Sometimes behaviour has to stop before you can look at its meaning. The more disruptive the behaviour, the clearer and firmer the boundaries must be. If it is still possible, it is advisable to set boundaries empathically. This means that you show that you realize that the behaviour is only an expression of something else and that it may become meaningful if we understand what is going on. With an empathic boundary, you put the perception of the inner world in the spotlight when you limit the behaviour. You show that you not only want the behaviour to stop, but also that you understand that this behaviour is there for a reason.

Phoebe, Anne, and Ruby
Anna and Ruby live together in a community and they are having a terrible fight. They are yelling and screaming at each other. Community worker Phoebe intervenes: 'I want you to stop this immediately. I can imagine a lot has happened between you, making you react to each other like that. I want to talk to you about that, so we can better understand why you react so

violently. But you have to stop saying such hurtful things, otherwise we won't be able to have such a conversation, and everyone will feel very bad about what happened.'

Phoebe limits the behaviour, but immediately refers to the world of inner experience behind the behaviour: 'I can imagine a lot has happened between you, making you react to each other like that.' She combines the limit setting of the behaviour with a focus on its underlying meaning. In addition, she is transparent about why the behaviour needs to stop: '. . . otherwise we won't be able to have such a conversation, and everyone will feel very bad about what happened.' If someone feels seen and understood in the reasons why he or she exhibits disruptive behaviour, the behaviour will decrease more quickly than if someone feels identified with that behaviour ('What a nasty girl you are!').

> Empathic limit setting demands a great deal of one's own mentalizing capacity. It requires—certainly in such hectic situations as the one Viraj and Phoebe had to deal with—that you are firm enough and still remain attuned. Do you have examples of this?

In a more equal relationship, such as a partner relationship, the empathic limit setting will often look somewhat different. Take the following example:

Jonathan and Kathleen are talking about the incident. By dwelling on what happened, their emotions become more and more heated. Kathleen starts making accusations, Jonathan gets very irritated because she only judges him on the incident. They start shouting louder and louder and stop listening to each other. Kathleen realizes that this is not what she wants, no matter how angry she is. She says: 'Let's stop this conversation. I'm too angry now and we say things that don't help. Let's talk again when we have cooled down.'

What Kathleen does here is essentially similar to what Viraj and Phoebe did: stop the unproductive behaviour in a state of poor mentalizing. This is needed to create space for mutual understanding. Note that Kathleen only succeeds in doing this because, during the argument, she realizes that she does not want this and that it will not help: her mentalizing is therefore already somewhat restored and that makes it possible for her to set boundaries.

Tip 5: Approach others with a basic mentalizing attitude

A basic mentalizing attitude means—as we already discussed in Chapter 2—that you always pay attention to both the behaviour that someone displays and the feelings, thoughts, needs, and expectations that lie behind it. Not just looking at Jonas as a naughty boy because he is very active, but as a boy who may become active out of a sense of fear when something scary happens in the classroom. Seeing Prisha not only as a big girl who helps the teacher and Sarah, but as a girl who seeks control by focusing on the other person, possibly from the need to get a grip on her own feelings of anxiety.

When you adopt a basic mentalizing attitude, you are genuinely curious about your own inner world and that of others: you want to understand the behaviour of the other person and yourself. At the same time, you realize that you can have all sorts of ideas about why someone does what he or she does, but that you can never know someone's inner world with certainty. You do not immediately draw conclusions. In short, you don't know anything for sure, but you do want to know.

> Think back to a time when you have felt misunderstood, for example in your relationship or at work. What made you feel misunderstood? Did you feel that the other person really listened to you? Did you feel that there was room for your perspective of the situation? What effect did that have on you in that situation?
>
> Think back to a moment when you did feel understood, when you had the space to tell your side of the story, when you felt that the other person really tried to understand you and was really interested in your thoughts, feelings, and needs. How did you feel then?

It is very nice when others approach you from such a basic mentalizing attitude. It often gives you the feeling that you matter, that your feelings and thoughts are allowed to be there. Conversely, it is often annoying when you feel that others have their opinions ready and there is no room for your story.

A basic mentalizing attitude starts from paying attention to the inner world. You can help yourself by asking yourself some questions, for example:

- Why is he or she saying this now? From what need?

- What moves him or her?
- Why does he or she react like this?
- What have I possibly done to make him or her feel this way? How does that make me feel?
- Has something happened to make him or her suddenly react like this?

By asking yourself these kinds of questions, you focus your attention beyond the behaviour to the experience behind it. From a basic mentalizing attitude you then enter into a conversation and ask the other person open questions. Sometimes it helps to put aside your own perspective or opinion for a moment and try to understand the situation purely from the point of view of the other person: What is he or she feeling, thinking, or experiencing now? Open questions help you to form a better picture of this.

The easiest way is to start such a conversation with questions about facts and events. These are not yet fully mentalizing and therefore require little mentalizing ability from the other person: What has happened? What is going on? Usually, the other person will start to tell a story, which may include aspects of their inner world. You can then question this further, for example with:

- Why do you think he or she reacted like that?
- What did you want to achieve by saying that?
- What was it about what he or she said that irritated you?
- What gets you so upset?
- How did you feel about him or her reacting like that?

Often questions about thoughts, about reasons for doing something, are easier to answer than questions about feelings. Don't be afraid to keep asking until you can really form a picture of how someone is thinking or feeling or experiencing a situation. You can pay attention to both the experiences of the event someone is telling about and what it is like to talk about it.

Nikita and Dina
Nikita lingers a bit after class. Dina, her mentor, notices that she wants to tell something. Nikita starts crying. She says that she is afraid to go home. Her father often has a bad temper when he drinks. Dina creates a space for Nikita to tell something about her father and the situation at home, but also asks her what it is like for her to talk about this. After all, by sharing this secret, a tensive situation is created in this contact, which is or can be emotionally meaningful for Nikita.

By engaging in such a conversation, others can help to understand how a certain event or situation touched someone and why he or she reacted in a certain way. Of course, adolescents and adults can say more about this than young children. With the latter, you may wish to focus on recognizing basic feelings within a specific context. You might also think more out loud with the child: 'Were you rather afraid when that happened, or rather angry?' In such a conversation Jonas would perhaps understand something about himself afterwards, like: 'When Sarah cries so loudly, I get scared and start to act wild.' When Jonas and those around him start to see this link, it can also have an impact on the image that he has of himself. He is no longer a naughty child, but a child who becomes wild when scared.

Finally, it is good to be on the lookout for different emotions in a conversation. For example, anger or irritation are emotions that often occur together with other emotions. However, these are often the emotions that you primarily experience, which means that it takes more time and reflection, for example in a conversation with another person, to realize that you are also sad or disappointed.

> This week, try to start a conversation with someone with a basic mentalizing attitude. Your goal is to form a picture of the other person's inner world by asking interested, open questions.

Tip 6: Offer emotional support to others

Good mentalizing is often lost when (painful) emotions are involved. You then experience those emotions too strongly or too truly (psychic equivalence mode: what I feel and think is true) or you become disconnected from your emotions (pretend mode: feeling empty, flat, and detached). Re-visiting those emotions and dwelling on them is not always easy. Especially if you have often felt not seen or understood when you were emotionally upset, this can be scary. It is very pleasant when someone supports you in this: what you feel is allowed to be there. Support can often be found in everyday words and phrases ('Oh, how annoying!' or 'How awful that must have been for you!' or 'Pooh, I can imagine that that upset you!').

There are many everyday situations that would go much easier if someone felt seen and supported in a certain way. Here's a simple example from the pandemic lockdown times of COVID-19:

A supermarket customer angrily lashes out at a cashier because there is no more toilet paper. The cashier is not in the mood for another angry customer, especially not because she is tired after a hard day's work and personally cannot help the fact that people are stockpiling. Nevertheless, she manages to remain calm: 'I understand that it is very annoying. I understand your frustration, because all those hoarders make me angry too. I'm sorry I can't help you now, but normally there will be enough stock tomorrow and I hope to see you at the checkout again with a packet of toilet paper!' The customer feels seen and validated in his frustration, and this eases his anger somewhat. He smiles and tells the cashier that he understands that she cannot do anything about it either, but that this was just the last straw for him.

Giving support means recognizing and validating someone's emotional experience. Validating means letting someone know that the emotion is allowed to be there, normalizing it within the context and indicating that you understand the effect of the situation on the person. Bear in mind that in order to validate properly, you need to really understand someone's experience or perception. Validation is not the same as simply telling someone that something is unpleasant or annoying. It means being able to put yourself in someone's shoes, to really understand their emotions or experience, and to use that understanding to normalize and support. We gave an example in Chapter 1. Olivia had become angry after she felt she was not allowed to participate in her group:

After observing the incident in the classroom, Christopher had a conversation with Olivia. As soon as Christopher had a good view of Olivia's inner world, he tried to mirror it by means of empathic validation: 'That sounds very sad, as if you really wanted to do your best, and when others did not seem to see it that way, it was very painful for you. I understand now that you felt trapped for a moment, that you saw no other way out than to get angry'.

Christopher explicitly describes the context (others do not see that Olivia is doing her best), Olivia's experience (being trapped, painful, sad) and the effect on her (getting angry). In turn, Olivia feels seen and heard and it created openness to look at her classmates and Christopher in a different way (epistemic trust). The quality of the relationship between Christopher and Olivia, but also between Olivia and her classmates, could subsequently improve because of this.

In order to provide support, it can sometimes help to find out what or how someone would like to be seen. How would that difficult student, client, or colleague like to be seen? How would your partner like to be recognized?

Tip 7: Take the lead in helping another person handle tension

If the tension is very high, you sometimes have to actively take the lead so that the situation does not get completely out of hand. Let's go back to the example of Callum and Finley.

Viraj, Finley, and Callum
Viraj has managed to calm things down, although he feels that there is still a hostile atmosphere between Callum and Finley. He doubts for a moment whether he will just let things be, but then realizes that there is a good chance that the scenario will repeat itself in no time. He decides to gather all the students. He says that he is glad that peace has returned, but that he notices that the tension is still in the air. 'I want to discuss with you where things went wrong. Is there anyone who wants to tell me what happened?' Callum immediately jumps in: 'Finley should just shut up more often.'

How to proceed? Viraj must show leadership. If he lets the conversation go on, Callum and Finley's mental state—and perhaps that of the rest of the class—will not recover and they will be at each other's throats again in no time. Viraj will first have to set limits to his behaviour. Afterwards, he can use the technique 'stop, rewind, and explore'. This technique helps you, when tension is running high, to return to the moment when the tension was not yet so high and mentalizing was still more or less effective.

Viraj intervenes immediately: 'I want everyone to stick to the agreements now. We have fifteen minutes, and, in that time, I demand that everyone does his best to stop cursing and really listen to each other, so that we can solve this. Callum and Finley, when you entered the classroom, I saw that you were still laughing. At that time, nothing seemed wrong. When did that change? What was the moment that this tension between you arose?' Viraj tries to pinpoint the start of the escalation: Things were going OK between you, then something happened and that eventually triggered the near-fight. Winston, who was a witness, says: 'I think Callum was sanding his tabletop and Finley said something about it. Then things got out of hand'. Viraj picks up on this: 'So, Winston, you think the immediate cause was Finley making a remark to Callum. Is that right, Callum? Was that the moment things got out of hand?' Callum replies: 'He had to tell me again that he could do it better.' Viraj mirrors: 'You got stuck and then Finley said something that you found very annoying, is that right?' Callum nods. 'What exactly made you so angry about what he said?' Callum answers: 'He said it in such an arrogant tone, as if he knows better.' Finley vehemently resists: 'That's not true, liar!'

So far, so good. Or almost. The 'stop, rewind, and explore' makes the beginning of arousal regulation possible. Very cautiously, something of the context in which Callum was affected emerges. We get an idea of his experience: apparently, he felt hurt by a remark of Finley and possibly he felt undermined by it. At the same time, you notice that the situation is still highly inflammable. Finley reacts agitatedly to Callum's interpretation of his remark. But the tension is not as high as before. Viraj can use a 'stop, listen, and look' here: he slows down the conversation and stands still by focusing on this transition.

Viraj intervenes again: 'Finley, wait a minute. What makes you say it like that, what makes you react like that?' To prevent the interaction between Callum and Finley, which has become somewhat regulated, from flaring up again, he picks up on the interaction that is taking place in the here-and-now. Finley responds: 'Callum says I was being arrogant, but that wasn't true. I saw that he took the wrong tool and wanted to help him.' Viraj backs up: 'Okay, you're responding because you think it's unfair that Callum calls your tone arrogant. If I understand you correctly, you were trying to give some advice. But, as I hear from Callum, he did not experience that remark as supportive, on the contrary. Something has clearly gone wrong between you. How did Finley's tip strike you then, Callum?'

What Viraj tries to do is to grasp the interaction, to pay attention to the experiences of both protagonists, to involve the others in the class, and to reconstruct step by step where things went wrong, by connecting and zooming in on the different twists and turns, both during the conflict and in the discussion. He slows down and tries to put a magnifying glass on the experiences of both in the interaction. In the first place he focuses on restoring Callum's and Finley's mentalizing about themselves. Only afterwards can he make them understand the other person's intentions. He validates and supports the perceptions of both. If the tension between the boys rises, he immediately stops the interaction and focuses their attention on what is happening between them in the here-and-now.

Not every teacher will feel comfortable discussing this in class in this way. However, what we want to illustrate is how you can address rising tensions in a mentalizing way. In the example of Viraj, this may require extreme effort and coordination, because the tension between these boys threatens to escalate quickly. But in many other situations, this technique can also be used to empathically limit behaviour, slow it down, and focus on the underlying experiences.

Tip 8: Validate the experience with someone in the psychic equivalence mode, making room for other perspectives

In the psychic equivalence mode, my truth is the truth: What I think and feel is true. Signal words are: always, never, everyone, nobody. Often someone in this mode evokes unpleasant feelings in others, such as frustration, irritation, anger, and powerlessness. We tend to convince the other person, to argue with him or her. Or we start walking on eggshells, because we notice that the other person does not tolerate it when we disagree with them.

Think back to Iris and Imogen. Iris notices that Imogen does not believe that things can change anymore and has actually given up hope of getting her life back on track. She could try to convince her: 'You can really do it, you have sorted your life out before, haven't you? You have so many talents!' What would be the effect on Imogen? Perhaps she would only think something like: Yes, but the situation was different then. Now I really can't manage.

If someone is in the psychic equivalence mode (Imogen: I am hopeless and there is no point in trying because I will keep failing anyway), then it's important in the first place to try to connect to how the other person experiences reality. When doing so, you make use of the basic mentalizing attitude. You ask questions, listen, support, and validate. You try to understand the other person's point of view, to understand how they think and feel inside. You validate empathically and thus mirror how you understand the other person. In doing so, you also trigger something of epistemic trust: 'He, she really seems to understand me.' From there, you can gradually stimulate curiosity to try to get someone to distance themselves from their own experience: 'I wonder how you came to the conclusion that it all makes no sense?' Or: 'I notice that I look at it somewhat differently.'

Iris, for example, can validate her unpleasant state of powerlessness in a conversation with Imogen: 'It seems very unpleasant to always have the idea that it makes no difference whether you do your best or not. I understand that such a feeling makes you want to give up at times. And the fact that you let things slide probably reinforces your feeling of powerlessness. I just wonder how you came to that conclusion, Imogen, that it makes no sense at all?' Or she could say: 'I now understand better why you often can't bring yourself to get started, Imogen. Still, I wonder if your assumption that it doesn't matter anyway is correct and if, by resigning yourself to it, you are not especially confirming yourself in your feelings of powerlessness. I know there have been periods in which you were much better at motivating yourself. So, it doesn't seem to me that you can't do it. It's just that you haven't been able to do it for a while, and maybe we should try together to understand what's behind that.'

Tip 9: Look for the underlying need of someone in a teleological mode

In a teleological mode, someone can only feel something 'mental' or 'emotional' when something tangible is done. Think back to Elizabeth and the nursery attendants from Chapter 3. She demanded an extensive written report every day, so that she could trust that her daughter was being well cared for. An oral report does not suffice. Trying to convince Elizabeth that the carers have taken good care of Ava might even be counterproductive. In the teleological mode, only what can be seen is real. The appeal to the other person is often experienced as very compelling. He or she feels manipulated, pressured, powerless, or angry. Yet, it is probably not Elizabeth's intention to manipulate. Her demand is understandable from her experience: if you can only trust your child's carers if they report extensively, then it is very threatening and frightening if they have not done so. Does this mean that the supervisors in this example should try harder to report more? No. It is an illusion that responding to the appeal will take away the underlying experiences. What is needed is that Elizabeth feels understood and validated in her needs. Why is it so important to her that everything is in the notebook? If we understand this, if we understand her need, then we understand why she is so upset when there is no report. At that moment we can better validate her needs, so that Elizabeth feels acknowledged. This recognition, feeling really seen in something that is 'vital' for her, might even give more confidence than the written reports.

Elizabeth and Dana

Elizabeth is once again upset when only a short report is noted down. Dana, one of the supervisors, talks to her: 'You know, Elizabeth, I often hear you ask for an extensive report and I would really like to think along with you about how we can meet this in all the hustle and bustle, but I do not yet understand why it is so important to you?' Elizabeth thinks for a moment: 'I just want to be sure that Ava is well looked after, and if you don't write that down, I don't know.' Elizabeth describes what it is like for her to take Ava to daycare. She is very scared of having to let go of taking care of Ava and trusting that others will do as well as she does. This helps Dana to understand her better. Dana then mirrors Elizabeth's needs: 'Of course I understand your concern about whether we are taking good care of Ava. As a mother, I would worry about that too. It is always somewhat scary to leave your child with others, especially when you don't know how she will be cared for. But I can really assure you that Ava is in good hands here. If you feel like it, you can stay a little longer, and you can get an idea of how we look after the children here.'

Dana tries to connect with the need behind the request for a written report. Elizabeth may have a need for reassurance. If Dana validates that need, it reduces the need for a concrete action.

> Do you have an example of such a teleological mode in your own personal or professional life? If you think about it, what could be the need behind that person's compelling question?

Tip 10: Connect someone in the pretend mode with emotions

In the pretend mode, words and feelings are disconnected. People talk 'about' themselves, not 'from within' themselves. They tell stories without really connecting with their emotional meaning. Sometimes they also feel flat and empty. Think back to Rachel, from Chapter 3, who talks to her team leader Lisa about this and that, while Lisa is worried about her and feels that Rachel is feeling very bad. Something happens that makes Lisa not answer her questions, maybe even forget why she started the conversation in the first place. When someone else is in pretend mode, the person you are talking to often loses interest along the way. The conversation doesn't really interest us, and we tend to get bored. This often results in a superficial conversation that is not really about anything.

It is not always easy to recognize the pretend mode. It is difficult not to get carried away in a conversation with someone in this mode. Sometimes, it can even sound as if someone has really figured things out. In the pretend mode, arousal is actually too low. You therefore need to raise the arousal if you really want to get back in touch with someone. Continuous questioning and focusing on the feelings (or the lack thereof) in the here-and-now help with this. You have to bite into the conversation like a pit bull.

> *Rachel and Lisa*
> *Lisa notices that Rachel is wandering off. She was worried about Rachel, and now she hears herself agreeing with her a little. She says, 'Rachel, stop for a minute. I was worried about you, and now that we are talking, I don't know how you are doing. It's like you're avoiding talking about it. I really want to know how you feel.' Rachel is startled, her eyes turn red immediately. Lisa reassures her: 'I really don't want to make you sad, Rachel, but I am just worried about you.' Rachel says: 'I don't really know how I am doing and that is quite scary.'*

Lisa 'grabs' Rachel: she stops the aimless talking and uses her observations to go to her emotion. This helps Rachel out of her pretend mode for a moment. When she connects with herself again, it is painful, frightening, or sad: there is a reason why she is disconnected. Then, support is often very welcome.

Summary

In this chapter, we have presented ten tips for restoring mentalization and to reconnect to the other, from which someone can once again experience epistemic trust. At the same time, the ten tips are not a cookbook or a set of skills that can be learned overnight. Effective mentalization is a basic attitude, and therefore the fifth tip is perhaps the most important. If we succeed in approaching each other with a basic mentalizing attitude, it will undoubtedly have a positive effect on the nature and quality of our interactions.

Perhaps you should let the previous chapter sink in for a while. What from this chapter do you want to take with you now?

9

Collaboration towards a mentalizing environment

We are all part of a social network or system and often even of different systems, depending on the roles we have. We are parents, children, partners, employees, colleagues, and so on. In a broad sense, you could say that we are part of different teams. We often have to work as a team, for example when we are raising children, doing a job for a client, teaching young people, or supporting clients. Teamwork, however, is complex. People differ and usually have different views on what should be the right thing to do. Everyone has different values and norms, but also different reaction styles. Sometimes various people have different experiences with the same person. A team member may have a very different contact with one colleague than with another. Or take a child who puts one parent on a pedestal while constantly rejecting the other, so both parents' experiences with their child differ. This can lead to friction. Our mentalizing in teams—whether a team of parents, teachers, therapists, or yet another team—can therefore regularly come under pressure.

This sometimes leads to dilemmas, because people desperately need such teams to maintain or restore a basic mentalizing attitude. After all, we do not always succeed in restoring our own mentalizing. Sometimes children, pupils, colleagues, or others get under our skin so much, or touch something so vulnerable in us, that it is difficult to recover our mentalizing on our own. Then we need others, others who are perhaps more distant, less affected, or who have a different perspective. We also saw this in the previous chapters. Take Erik from Chapter 2, who after a short conversation with Hannah begins to realize why Nathan affects him so much. It is therefore important that we not only create a mentalizing environment around our children, students, and clients, but also around the parents, teachers, and caregivers involved. They can only help others when they have recovered their mentalizing. This chapter therefore focuses on the importance of

The Power of Mentalizing. Joost Hutsebaut, Liesbet Nijssens, and Miriam van Vessem, Oxford University Press.
© Joost Hutsebaut, Liesbet Nijssens, Miriam van Vessem 2023. DOI: 10.1093/oso/9780198880677.003.0009

colleagues, partners, and other close people in creating and maintaining a mentalizing environment.

> Think about the teams you are part of. Which do you feel comfortable in, and in which do you feel less so? Which teams help you in your contact with your children, pupils, and clients? Which ones might make this difficult?

Cooperation problems

If a team does not function as a team, it can lead to various problems. Splitting is one of them. Splitting often occurs when arousal is high. The team is torn apart into two or more parts: there are irreconcilable differences of opinion that soon lead to an unbalanced and inconsistent approach. Between parents, this is sometimes most obvious: father and mother have different opinions about the upbringing. If they do not see eye to eye, this also influences the children. For example, children play the parents off against each other or show that they prefer one parent to the other. A divorce in particular can create an unfavourable parenting situation.

> *Harriet and Hugh*
> *Harriet and Hugh have been separated for some time. They have somewhat different ideas about the upbringing of their daughter, Gwen. Hugh is more liberal than Harriet. These differences of opinion played in the background, but never led to open discussions. But now that Gwen has a boyfriend, there is friction. Hugh allows her boyfriend to sleep over, but Harriet thinks she is too young for that. The result is that Gwen invites her boyfriend to her father's house. Her mother has no say in the matter.*

Another common problem is that in a team, some opinions become too dominant, and others tend to disappear into the background. As a result, potentially valuable insights are lost. This is what happens in Erik's team of teachers. Dominant voices say that you must be strict and firm with problem kids at school, leaving little room for a different approach.

These processes usually occur when (1) there are strong emotions involved and (2) the frameworks and agreements are less clear. Parents need to make agreements about bedtimes, mobile phone use, homework, and dozens of other things. If the agreements about this are unclear, this can exacerbate the differences. In a team, agreements must be made about how to deal with transgressive behaviour, how to be accessible, how to handle crises…Structure provides predictability and clarity. At the same time, it is an illusion that you can control all behaviour with structure and rules. In a family, class, or community, children and young people will regularly exhibit problematic behaviour and provoke emotional reactions from the adults around them.

Steven, Danny, and Helen
Francesca lives in a children's home. She is regularly cheeky to the supervisors and always keeps them at a distance. What the caretakers see is a big, cheeky, tough girl. In the group, others are often afraid of her. If you have Francesca against you, she will steamroll you. Very occasionally, some supervisors see a different side. Then she is suddenly very vulnerable and sad. At those times she feels like a failure, and she is afraid that nobody likes her.

The team does not know what to do. Opinions are divided. Steven and Danny think she should be transferred to another home, for her own good. They think Francesca belongs in a mental healthcare institution, where she can get professional help for her condition. Helen objects. She emphasizes that Francesca has been rejected so many times in her life that transferring her now will only repeat those traumas. She sees a very different side, namely a vulnerable girl who, behind the angry outside appearance, is very sad and afraid. She thinks—but she doesn't say so—that Steven and Danny are approaching Francesca in the wrong way. The rest of the team keeps a low profile. Sometimes the atmosphere in the team can become unpleasant when Helen goes against Steven and Danny, who seem to take sides. The other members of the team feel ambivalent and hesitate; they recognize something of what Helen calls attachment trauma, but they also agree with Steven and Danny that Francesca needs specialist help.

> If you work in social work or education, do you recognize this? That certain pupils or clients evoke different opinions and emotions from different team members? Maybe even in a family: that a child is experienced very differently by both parents? What is the effect of this on the team or the parent couple? How does the team or the parent couple deal with this, and what do you think the effect of this is on the pupil, the client, or the child?

Francesca evokes a lot of empathy and sympathy with some workers, like Helen, while with others, like Danny and Steven, she evokes irritation, powerlessness, and rejection. Even though there may be agreements in the institute about Francesca's behaviour, these cannot prevent Francesca's disruptive behaviour. It is often these kinds of strong emotions that lead to splits in teams. If a parent feels rejected because a child wants to be put to bed by the other parent, this may lead to the tendency to counter this behaviour in a stern tone of voice: 'You shouldn't whine, I'll just put you to bed!' If the other parent feels the effect of this on the child, he or she might actually take the child's side and that is how you lose each other as parents.

In Francesca's case, you can also imagine Helen defending her and minimizing her disruptive behaviour, while Danny and Steven emphasize the latter and have less eye for their client's vulnerable side. Helen does not pay enough attention to the effect Francesca has on her colleagues and on the community, while she does mentalize Francesca well. Danny and Steven, for their part, mentalize too little about Francesca, while they do think about the effects she has on others. Neither party has a monopoly on the truth, not even Helen, despite the fact that she feels close to Francesca. The effect of this split is obvious: there is a good chance that Francesca will allow herself to be guided exclusively by Helen and will only show Helen her vulnerable side. While it is this vulnerable side that gives others the opportunity to connect with her. This will undoubtedly strengthen Helen in her idea that Francisca really should not be sent away from the group. She will behave more hostile towards Danny and Steven, which will only confirm their opinion: there is no way to deal with Francesca, she disturbs the group atmosphere.

Also, when we ourselves have less mental space, and therefore less eye and attention for the needs and experiences of others, we will easily lose the connection with each other, leading to non-helpful and non-mentalizing interactions.

> *Kathleen is home after a hard day's work. David, her husband, is busy preparing the supper. Their little daughter Anne approaches Kathleen, happy that mummy is finally home, and begs to play a game, hanging on to her trousers. Kathleen can't stand it and tells Anne to leave her alone for a while. Anne starts to cry loudly. This disturbs David, who has been working hard himself and is also cooking for the family. He remarks irritably that Kathleen should do something too. Kathleen then explodes. Anne cries softly on the sofa.*

How can we help each other in such situations? As partners, co-educators, and as colleagues? In the rest of this chapter, we discuss strategies that parents, teachers, or care workers can use to help each other maintain or restore their mentalizing. The goal is for the team of parents, teachers, and caregivers to function more effectively: as one team, as a mentalizing environment around the child.

Tip 1: Agree on a vision

It all starts with a vision of what you want to achieve as a team and how you want to achieve it, which values and standards you base this on. It is important to talk about this with each other and to make clear agreements. Rules are not there for the sake of rules, but for the values and standards they serve. In a community group, for example, you can agree that everyone eats at the same time, because you think this is an important way to promote solidarity in the group and approach a family climate. In a family, you can agree not to take the mobile phone into the rooms at night, to promote sleep. Such agreements create a framework of expectations, a structure that reflects the values that you as a family, institution, or school stand behind. Precisely because agreements refer to a vision or value, they are also easy to explain. Avoid rules that you cannot explain: why? Therefore! This is how we do it here!

> *Today, Edson is on evening duty in the crisis unit. Things have often been unsettled lately. There are several clients who are regularly in a crisis. He is a little apprehensive about the evening, also because he is working with Philippa. She is a lot older, and she often goes in with her guns blazing he thinks. She is convinced that clients shouldn't be overprotected. Edson feels differently about that. Not that he wants to overprotect them, but one can have a conversation, right? Because Philippa is older, however, he does not dare to go against her.*

Edson and Philippa do not agree on the approach. They may have different values when dealing with clients. Maybe he is more on the side of contact and relationship, from where he actively tries to approach to clients. Maybe Philippa is more on the side of autonomy and own responsibility. It becomes difficult for them when these values have to be brought together, for example when they are on duty together. Who is right? Maybe both. The point here is: if they do not discuss this and form a common vision, there is a risk that they will approach things very differently. This will create unpredictability and thus insecurity, especially in a crisis unit. Of course, differences are allowed, but too many differences make you vulnerable as a team.

Is your team (parents, teachers, counsellors) on the same page? Do you agree on the vision, the values, and the standards? About the rules and the agreements that follow from these? About what and what not? What's the effect?

Tip 2: Ensure safety

A clear vision of values and a corresponding framework does not solve everything. Within that framework, a safe and open atmosphere is needed, so that you can come together when cross-border issues do arise. Think of Francesca, but also of Nathan, who challenges Erik in class (see Chapter 2). Promoting mentalizing in teams therefore also requires safety. So that you can stop and reflect on what you feel and think about yourself and others. So that you can talk to each other without emotions being immediately swept off the table and so that some people keep what affects them and what they think to themselves. In short, it is about adopting a basic mentalizing attitude towards each other. Not looking for a solution straight away, but first dwelling on the emotions and needs involved. In teams, key figures such as directors and supervisors play an important role in creating this safety.

> *Lewis, Philippa, and Edson*
> *Lewis is the head of the department where Philippa and Edson work. He appreciates them both, but also sees that they are from a different generation and have a different style. He has noticed that Edson feels more insecure when Philippa is present. Conversely, he can also imagine that it's sometimes confrontational for Philippa to notice that a lot of clients feel so comfortable with Edson and ask for him when they're both working. He decides to talk to Philippa and Edson.*
>
> *Lewis opens the conversation: 'Philippa and Edson, you both know how much I appreciate you. However, I can also see that there are differences between you, and I sometimes have the impression that this causes tension between you.' He gives both time and space to think about this.*

Lewis sees what is going on and tackles it instead of letting things happen. He creates a safe space for the conversation. First, he connects with both of them (not coincidentally by calling them both by name, an ostensive cue) and then he does not focus on the differences in behaviour and style, but on the perception they have of each other, so that they can both mentalize better about each other and about their cooperation. Moreover, he does this from sincere appreciation for both and from acceptance of their differences. By entering a conversation in this way, Philippa and Edson become more aware of the impact their differences have on each other and of the effect this has on their cooperation.

Tip 3: Recognize ineffective mentalizing in each other

If we want to help each other recover mentalizing, it is important that we immediately recognize and pick up on signs of ineffective mentalizing. If poor mentalizing remains undetected, it is likely to disrupt interactions.

Bart, Jacky, and Maria
Bart comes grumbling into the staffroom, where his colleague Maria is having a cup of coffee. He is irritated. Jacky has been acting difficult for a whole school year. She is a loose cannon. He has addressed her countless times, but all she does is look at him haughtily. As if he consists of air. He feels as if she is humiliating him in front of the class. His colleague Maria doesn't understand Bart's irritation. Jacky doesn't give her a hard time. Okay, she put her in her place at the beginning of the school year; maybe Bart should try that?

If Maria does not pay attention to the poor mentalizing in Bart, she will probably not be able to help him restore contact with Jacky. For example, she might distract Bart by broaching another subject, because she does not know how to deal with his irritations, which she does not understand. Or she might respond from her lack of understanding that this is only happening in his class and that he should think about his own role. Or maybe she wants to help Bart but does so with well-intentioned advice from her own perspective: 'Put her in her place, that helped me in my class. After that I never had a problem with Jacky again.' Chances are, however, that none of the above will help Bart. They will probably not help him to restore his own mental state, which would further worsen his interaction with Jacky. After all, poor mentalizing evokes poor mentalizing, which leads to missed opportunities for recovery. If Bart is irritated by Jacky's behaviour and cannot place or handle his irritation, he will be more likely to react based on this irritation. He will approach Jacky more negatively, speak to her with more charge, and see her behaviour more quickly as confirmation of her attempts to make him look foolish. Bart may think he is not showing his irritation. However, there is a good chance that some of his irritation seeps through into how he approaches Jacky and that Jacky senses this. Consequently, she may see Bart as a 'tough, difficult' teacher, leading her to respond with even more obstinacy and aloofness.

Selma, Libby, and Jasmine

It has been a busy day at the group home. Selma has been on her own and had her hands full with Jasmine. Jasmine was constantly asking her attention and was quite cheeky the whole day. Selma did not feel she could send Jasmine away. She was afraid that this would only make things worse. Therefore, she held back her irritation and tried to tolerate Jasmine as much as she could. At the transfer to the evening shift, she blows off steam: 'Jasmine bothered me all day. She did nothing but ask for negative attention. It is never enough with that child!' Libby, who has the evening shift, can already predict how things will go this evening. But she won't let this happen! She will immediately make clear to Jasmine that she won't tolerate this kind of behaviour.

Libby is contaminated by Selma's poor mentalizing. It can be predicted that Libby, from the irritation she already feels, will seek contact in a way that is unpleasant for Jasmine, who will most probably show exactly the same behaviour as with Selma. But what if Libby had noticed in time that Selma did not mentalize well anymore about Jasmine?

At the transfer to the evening shift, Selma blows off steam: 'Jasmine bothered me all day. She did nothing but ask for negative attention. It is never enough with that child!' Libby—who has the evening shift—notices that Selma is so affected by the contact with Jasmine that she cannot mentalize about her anymore. Libby supports Selma: 'Selma, I have the impression that you have had a really hard time on your own today. And apparently, Jasmine has done something that has made your day even harder? What has she done that bothers you so much?'

Libby recognizes Selma's ineffective mentalizing in her unsubtle statements and irritations. She supports Selma, but also tries to help her recover her mentalizing. This can be done by first connecting with the experience of Selma and with what has happened between Jasmine and her. If Libby does not do this, there is a big chance that when Selma runs into Jasmine during a next shift, they will both quickly get stuck in non-helpful interactions again. So, by helping Selma to mentalize about Jasmine again, she not only helps herself and Jasmine for that evening, but also Selma for the next shift.

How can others recognize that you are not mentalizing as well as you should? And what are the signs that you recognize in teammates who are important to you? Who starts talking in an unsubtle way? Who becomes very rational? Who fills in too many details? Who draws conclusions too quickly?

Tip 4: Help each other understand emotions

Bart and Selma's emotions show us the effect that someone else's behaviour can have on us. If we do not regulate these emotions but push them away, or even worse, if we react based on these unregulated emotions, this will often backfire. Sometimes we think it is 'professional' to push away or merely tolerate unwanted or negative feelings that we experience in relation to our clients or students, for example. Or that it is better to let differences of opinion with partners or friends blow over. This is often not true. If you are helped to understand and process your own emotion, you are better equipped to re-engage with the other person. This is confirmed by a great deal of research showing that therapists who do something constructive with the negative emotions that they experience in the contact with a client to achieve better treatment results. Suppressing these negative emotions prevents them from damaging the contact, but actively introducing and handling them makes the contact constructive. The same applies to parents: parents who are better able to handle their negative emotions will show less behaviour that disturbs the interaction with their child. If you want to prevent emotions from escalating, it is important to be able to handle these emotions. You do this by consciously experiencing them and giving them meaning: What exactly do I feel and why?

> Do you have pupils, colleagues, or clients with whom you have negative feelings? Irritation? Powerlessness? Maybe you think they are overreacting? That they exaggerate? Maybe you sometimes experience such unpleasant emotions towards your own children? What do you do with these feelings?

Within this process of giving meaning, team members can play an incredibly valuable and important role. What you can do as another parent or colleague, for example, when you notice that mentalizing is under pressure, is helping to understand and digest the underlying emotions. A first step in this can be to name what you notice in the other person, as Libby did during the transfer with Selma. Then you can ask your colleague or partner questions to understand what it was that made him or her unable to mentalize properly. Often, recounting the chain of events that preceded ineffective mentalizing is a first step towards regaining effective mentalizing. Perhaps most important, but possibly also most tensive, is to pay attention to the emotional impact of the interaction on the person.

Libby lets Selma talk about why she has had such a hard time with Jasmine. She supports her: 'Gee, Selma, Jasmine didn't make it easy for you today.' But she also lets Selma think about the effect Jasmine has had on her: 'Selma, do you know what really touched you today in the contact with Jasmine? What effect did she have on you today by behaving this way?' Selma thinks: 'She annoyed me so much. She kept searching for me, as if she needed me. And when I tried to do right by her, she always got angry.' Libby encourages Selma to reflect further: 'It sounds like you really did your best to help her today, that maybe she asked that of you, but for some reason it didn't work out? How did it feel, that this turned out this way?' Selma reflects further: 'It felt like I failed. Actually, most of the time I like Jasmine and we do get along, but now she just wouldn't let me be there for her. It actually made me insecure. Did I do something wrong?'

Selma's mentalizing will only recover when she gets a grip on the emotions she experienced in relation to Jasmine. Just telling her what happened is not enough to restore her mentalizing. Only when Selma can really slow down and reflect on how Jasmine has touched her, can she look at Jasmine differently. Libby, for her part, does not go straight for her goal ('What do you feel?'), but has an eye for Selma's vulnerable mental state after her shift. She supports Selma, mirrors what it must have been like for her and thus creates safety. The fact that today things have gone badly between Selma and Jasmine, does not change the trust Libby has in Selma as a colleague. This safety and trust give Selma the security to really mentalize about herself and her emotions.

Let's take a moment to return to Bart, who enters the teachers' room irritated and pours his guts out about Jacky. Suppose Maria does what she probably does more often in such situations: She sympathizes with Bart and agrees with him that Jacky is going too far, that this is a matter for the management. Maybe that helps Bart for a moment, and he doesn't have to doubt himself, but it won't help him in his interaction with Jacky. Nor is it any help to Bart when Maria tells him what to do: 'You just have to be tough on that girl.' More than that, this can be irritating for Bart or perhaps even strengthen his insecurity. There is a big chance that Bart won't feel understood and supported as a result. Bart will only be really able to benefit from Maria's advice if he has the impression that she really understands what it is like for him in his interaction with Jacky. This has to do with epistemic trust (see Chapter 6): only when Maria really understands me and really understands what I am up against with Jacky, her insights or advice on how to tackle this will be helpful. How could Maria do that? She can first help him to understand what he is experiencing in relation to Jacky's behaviour. Maria could acknowledge Bart's emotion and ask him what exactly happened: 'He Bart, bad class with Jacky? What happened?' This gives Bart the chance to talk about Jacky's irritating behaviour, who kept pretending he was nothing but air to her and how powerless that made him feel. Maria could support him: It is very sad he felt this way during that lesson. She could go on to ask what exactly Jacky did that made him feel this way. She helps him to better understand what it was exactly in Jacky's behaviour that made him so frustrated. One step further: What exactly did it evoke in him? What affected him so? This can help Bart gain more insight into his highly charged emotions in this interaction. For example, he can talk about feeling powerless and angry when she does not allow herself to be controlled, but that he also feels uncomfortable and perhaps even belittled when other classmates watch while she does this.

> Can you talk to each other in your team in such a way? Do you think you can introduce some of that culture? What could you and your team gain from this?

Tip 5: Help each other consider other perspectives

Helping your partner or colleague to understand something of the emotion that the behaviour causes in him or her is an indispensable starting point. But it is not enough. If Bart remains convinced that Jacky is pretending he is air to her, he will continue to arm himself against her. If Selma keeps thinking that Jasmine attracts and repels her or wants to make her feel that she can't do anything right, then she is not (sufficiently) helped. And if David doesn't pay attention to the hard day Kathleen has had, or if Kathleen only feels attacked and doesn't think about the fact that David also had a busy and tiring day, they will neither help each other nor their little daughter Anne to find peace again.

Understanding your own emotion in relation to the other person's behaviour is a starting point for rethinking why the other person is behaving in this way and what you yourself might be doing to generate this effect. Here, colleagues or partners can help. They can help you think again about the emotions, needs, or desires from which the other person is displaying this behaviour. This way, an open mind is created again. Bart will only be able to break through the impasse with Jacky if he can understand something of the mental state behind her behaviour. Maria can help Bart by getting a grip on the interaction: Why is Jacky behaving this way and what is Bart possibly doing to make Jacky behave this way? To this end, she could ask him whether Jacky exhibits this behaviour all the time or whether it is intermittent. She could also ask at which moments Jacky behaves in a disruptive or rebellious manner, and whether Bart has any ideas about the mental state from which she exhibits this behaviour. Perhaps Bart will find out that she misbehaves, especially when she must do something she is not good at. Maria can ask Bart for ideas about the meaning behind her behaviour: From what feeling or need does Jacky display this behaviour in these situations? Perhaps Bart will think that she may feel very insecure at such times. Maybe she is displaying behaviour that makes him feel insecure precisely at those moments when she feels insecure herself. Maria can then go on to ask what effect this has on him, what he does at those moments and what the effect of this might be on her. Is there perhaps something Bart does unintentionally that makes her feel even more insecure? Bart might recognize that when he notices a change in Jacky's attitude, he quickly starts to arm himself and become stricter, and therefore perhaps less accessible to the questions that might help her tackle the task.

Of course, Bart does not know what is going on in Jacky's head. However, he will approach her differently if there is again some flexibility in how he looks at her. If she's just the annoying teenager who keeps pretending him to be air for her, the interaction is guaranteed to break down again and again. If he can imagine that she might have other reasons for behaving this way, he can approach her with more openness. When Bart has Jacky in his classroom again after the conversation with Maria, there is a real chance that he will behave slightly differently. Perhaps he will be a little more attentive to her potential vulnerability. Maybe Jacky feels this, and something can change in the interaction between them.

But now back to Selma and Libby.

Libby helped Selma to understand better what had touched her in her contact with Jasmine. She felt she was failing. She wanted to help Jasmine so much, but felt she could not, which had affected her deeply. Now that Selma is mentalizing well again, Libby can help her by investigating with her what might have been going on with Jasmine that day. This not only helps Selma, but also Libby, who still has the evening shift ahead of her. She asks Selma: 'Can you think of anything that might have caused Jasmine to behave so erratically today? Did something happen earlier today, or yesterday?' This sets Selma thinking: 'Now that you mention it. Normally Jasmine's mother would have picked her up this weekend, but she cancelled this morning. I don't know why her mother didn't come, but it's quite possible that this has affected Jasmine very much?' 'What do you think it has done to her, as you know her?' Selma continues: 'I can well imagine that Jasmine will start to wonder what she has done wrong. Whether she is such a worthless daughter that her mother does not even come to pick her up.'

Because Selma's mentalizing has been restored, she can also think again about Jasmine's mental state. She allows other perspectives: Jasmine is no longer just a girl who has been making her blood boil all day, but also someone who has felt very bad and rejected today. Perhaps not so very different from how Selma ended the shift.

> In the example of Selma and Libby, we have written two scenarios: without and with recovery of mentalizing. What is the effect of both scenarios on Jasmine, Selma, and Libby? What is the added value of the recovery of mentalizing for Selma's work in the group home? Do you agree that Libby can help Selma to 'be a better version of herself'?

Maybe some people think that it is up to students and clients to behave properly and that it is not the task of teachers and social workers to think about this. And yet, that is exactly why we wrote this book: We believe that it is up to us as parents, teachers, community workers, and therapists to help these children, adolescents, or clients to regulate themselves and their relationships. It is our conviction that Jacky will be better able to regulate her own behaviour if she understands better why she does what she does, not only to Bart, but perhaps to many more adults and peers who might evoke some insecurity in her. It is also our belief that if Jacky is more successful in this, she will learn more from Bart's lessons and that Bart will ultimately have to expend less energy in limiting her behaviour. It is our conviction that Selma's next shift will go better with Jasmine when she is once again in touch with the mental state behind her behaviour. And that she can only achieve this by better understanding Jasmine's effect on herself. In short, it is our belief that it is up to parents, teachers, community supervisors, and therapists to start this process of change. This does not mean that we should simply tolerate the behaviour of Jacky or Jasmine. Look at the example of Naomi and Rob, next.

Tip 6: Respect all perspectives and opinions

In a team, different team members usually have different ideas. It would be a shame not to make use of them, also because every perspective may contain some truth. Or better: Nobody has a monopoly on truth. Think back to the example of Francesca: Helen is 'correct' that there is a lot of pain and perhaps fear of rejection behind Francisca's behaviour, and that sending her away is almost re-traumatizing. But Danny and Steven are also right: What Francesca does is not acceptable and makes the community unsafe. Especially when there are strong emotions involved, opinions and perspectives tend to separate, to cause a split. Especially then, it is very important to question everyone and get all perspectives on the table.

> *Naomi*
> *There is a theft in the classroom. It's not the first time. Last time it was a necklace, now an iPhone suddenly disappeared. After a search, it turned out that Gregg was behind it. At first, he denied it vehemently, but eventually he did admit it. The school wants to draw a line: Should Gregg be suspended? Expelled from school? Should he get detention? Offer apologies? Do a restorative punishment? It is complicated by the fact that Gregg's father died last year. Moreover, his father was not a nice guy: he had a criminal record himself. In the team of teachers, opinions are divided. The director, Naomi, leads the discussion and makes sure that everyone's point of view, opinions, and ideas are put on the table. She even asks the secretary, who is taking notes, for her ideas.*

Unfortunately, there is often a fight over who is right. Parents get into conflict with each other about the upbringing. Team members try to convince each other they are right. It makes more sense to try to understand the different perspectives. In a team meeting of a treatment team, it can be useful to explicitly check whether all perspectives of all team members are on the table. Team members who have not yet said much may be explicitly invited to do so. It is often very fruitful to question new staff members because they often think from a new and fresh perspective. Parents can also question each other: How do you see this? What do you think we should do?

Tip 7: Investigate differences

When people have different perspectives, it is not a question of who is more dominant or who is right. What is more important is to examine differences in perspectives: How can we understand those differences? Why do we look at this so differently? Why do *you* think this will help? Genuine interest in differences is the best way to arrive at solutions. In fact, it promotes mentalizing about differences. When emotions run high in a heated discussion, it can sometimes be appropriate to write out the different opinions and views on a board and note where the main differences lie.

Naomi

Naomi makes a diagram of the different opinions. Some teachers are very out-spoken: the school cannot tolerate this behaviour. Students who steal make it unsafe for other students and threaten the general school climate. Not acting repressively sends a bad signal to the rest. Some other teachers emphasize the difficult period Gregg is going through. Maybe he identifies with his father, which would not be strange since he died recently. Especially now, the school should not let him down too, then he is a goner.

The different views can be understood from the standpoint you take, the headmaster observes. If you take the school's point of view, the behaviour must stop, and repressive action must be taken. If, on the other hand, you take Gregg's point of view, there is more room for understanding and tolerance. She asks the critical teachers how they view the hypothesis that Gregg espe-cially misses his father. And what they think the effect would be on Gregg if they sent him away. To the other teachers, she asks how they see the impact of this behaviour on the school climate. And what the effect would be if they just let him stay. This way, Naomi tries to come to a coherent measure in which all per-spectives are represented.

A measure or sanction that has been well-mentalized will usually be of higher quality than an intervention that has been badly mentalized. It is then less likely to be inspired by a private emotion or by only one aspect of the 'truth'. In Gregg's example, Naomi therefore does justice to all perspectives: both to that of the teachers who point out the need to monitor the school climate, and to that of the other teachers who sense that too harsh a measure might dispro-portionately harm Gregg.

Naomi invites Gregg and his mother for a talk. She explains to them that it is im-portant for the school that the climate is safe. Because Gregg has threatened that safety, a sanction will be imposed on him to give a clear signal that this behaviour will not be tolerated. At the same time, she tells them that the school is worried about Gregg and that they have noticed that he is not quite himself since the death of his father. The school wonders if the stealing has something to do with this. Naomi thinks with his mother and Gregg about what the school can do to help Gregg, but also advises him to look for external help. Gregg feels relieved. He was afraid of being kicked out of school, especially now his mother is having such a hard time. Perhaps he is even more relieved because the school has thought about him and noticed that things are not going well. He also understands that stealing is wrong.

Summarizing the above, the rule in teams would be: Monitor the process, not just the content. The process is about the form in which the discussion or consultation takes place (how it proceeds), the content about what the various content-related opinions are. If the process by which parents, a teaching team or a treatment team arrive at a joint approach to a problem is better, likely the approach itself will also be better and more balanced. If the form is good, the content is almost always better.

In larger teams, this can sometimes be a challenge. A useful strategy is to appoint a process supervisor in discussions. This person does not take part in the content of the discussion but monitors the mentalizing process. He or she intervenes when that process falters, for example when unsubstantiated statements are made, certain perspectives are not addressed, some team members are conspicuously absent from the discussion, decisions are made hastily, or major differences of opinion remain unresolved. The supervisor intervenes by sharing his or her observations and asking exploratory questions. 'I notice that Mustafa and Hannah have a very different point of view; maybe we should try to understand that difference a bit better first.' 'I have the impression that you still have double feelings about this client, Khadija.' The supervisor thus initiates the recovery of mentalizing. This also prevents poor mentalizing from contaminating other colleagues and leading to behaviour that further disrupts interactions. The role of the supervisor can be taken on by the discussion leader (i.e., the director, the directing clinician, the head nurse, etc.), but often this is not even necessary and sometimes it is just not practical. It can then also be a rotating task within the team.

Restore mental health within teams:
- Agree on a vision.
- Establish safety.
- Recognize ineffective mentalizing in each other.
- Help each other understand emotions.
- Help each other consider other perspectives.
- Respect all perspectives and opinions.
- Explore differences.

How do you think you can ensure in your team that the mentalizing process and the discussion in the team are monitored? What is needed for this?

Summary

In this chapter some tips are given to improve the functioning of a team. A team can be understood as a couple of parents, a team of teachers, a team of community workers, a group of friends, a treatment team. Everywhere, when people work together, you have to deal with differences. Differences can have a positive impact on performance if there is room for them and justice is done to the different points of view. If the differences become too big and the positions polarized, they can have a negative effect: team members will find themselves on opposite sides of the table, which can easily lead to inconsistent and therefore confusing task performance.

Our basic assumption is that substantive functioning improves as the underlying process becomes more mentalized. This requires safety in the team and a basic mentalizing attitude from all team members, in which they are open to and curious about their own feelings, needs, and meanings as well as those of others.

10

Vulnerabilities and resilience in adolescence

Puberty is not a pleasant time for everyone. About three-quarters of all psychological problems that people will develop in their lives have already developed by the end of puberty. Puberty is also seen by most parents and educators as the most difficult phase in parenting. At the same time, it is a pivotal phase that determines further development. In this chapter, we will look at the development of mental health problems, the role of puberty, and how we as parents, educators, or supervisors can support adolescents who are vulnerable.

An important question for people working with children is what exactly they want to teach them. A more specific question for parents and educators is when they can let go of a child, and let them step into the world independently.

Maybe you have children of your own. What do you wish for your child when they are sixteen, eighteen, and twenty-three? What would make you proud? When would you feel that your job as a parent is done?

Perhaps it is important for parents to be able to trust that their child can stand on their own two feet. That they can shape their own lives and deal with the opportunities, but also the setbacks, that come their way. It is great when your child has a good job and a beautiful family, but perhaps it is even more important that you can trust that he or she will also be able to stand on his or her own two feet when that job is abolished or when something difficult happens in the family. Ultimately, parents want their child to be resilient in life. But how do you help a child to become resilient? And what can you do when a child is very vulnerable?

The Power of Mentalizing. Joost Hutsebaut, Liesbet Nijssens, and Miriam van Vessem, Oxford University Press.
© Joost Hutsebaut, Liesbet Nijssens, Miriam van Vessem 2023. DOI: 10.1093/oso/9780198880677.003.0010

Puberty

A lot of research shows that parents find parenting most difficult when their child is in puberty. Take Alice, who struggles with her daughter Kiki.

Alice and Kiki
Alice is worried about her fourteen-year-old daughter Kiki. She has changed since last school year, according to Alice. Before then, Kiki was always open and energetic. She could sometimes be very sad when something was going on at school, but she was always open about it. That gave Alice confidence. This has not been the case for a year now. Kiki often withdraws into her room and reacts irritably whenever Alice tries to start up a conversation with her. Alice attributed this to puberty, although she did not feel comfortable with it. Last week she discovered mixed drinks in Kiki's room. She wanted to say something but didn't know how to handle it. Should she say anything at all? Their contact is already difficult and Alice does not want to create even more tension. Maybe it doesn't mean anything? Maybe Kiki will grow out of it? You often hear about teenagers going through a difficult time, don't you?

Maybe you recognize yourself in Alice, you also have a son or daughter in puberty and sometimes you do not know whether you should worry or not. Or maybe you have children like Kiki in your class or in the community. We feel that something is going on, but when should we really worry? Isn't it normal for adolescents to go through a depression sometimes? Hormones and so on?

Lex is worried about Bill, a boy in his mentor class. Bill is now sixteen years old. He has gone through a huge growth spurt in the last year: until last year, he was small, still a child really, and now suddenly he is a man. But Bill has also started to behave differently. He has never been much of an open book, but recently he seems to withdraw even more. He often sits alone in class and doesn't seem to connect with others in the schoolyard either. It's as if he can't find a way to behave himself anymore. Bill's parents split up two years ago and his father immediately found a new girlfriend. Lex isn't sure what effect this has had on Bill. Is he just a late adolescent, is he struggling with the situation at home, or is there perhaps more to it?

The examples of Kiki and Bill illustrate that puberty can be a difficult period. The resilience of children is often severely tested. It is no coincidence that this is also the period in which vulnerable children experience increasing difficulties. This is reflected in the figures. Especially serious mental illnesses manifest themselves for the first time in this stage of development. Those who get through puberty fairly smoothly have relatively little chance of developing serious mental health problems later in life. It makes our task as a parent, counsellor, or teacher important, but sometimes also very difficult.

How do you remember your own puberty? Who helped you during this period?

When we described the development of mentalizing, attachment, and epistemic trust, we talked a lot about what happens in the first years of life. We discussed how important it is to be able to trust that your caregivers are available, and to be able to count on them to recognize and respond to your needs and desires. The countless experiences children have in their relationships with parents and other caregivers create a basic understanding of who they are and what they can expect from others. With that foundation, children enter primary school at the age of six. They are ready to learn from and play with others. The primary school period is usually the calmest for parents. If there are any worries at all, they are often minor. Until puberty sets in, that is.

Not all adolescents are difficult or cause us problems, far from it. But if there is a vulnerability in the child's foundation, puberty will usually magnify it. Sometimes puberty is called the psychological birth of an individual. And just as the biological birth can be a stumbling block for physically vulnerable children, puberty can be a stumbling block for psychologically vulnerable children. This has a lot to do with all the changes and challenges that adolescents face.

Kiki was always a temperamental child. Alice remembers that, as a toddler, she could not be kept in her playpen. Kiki always wanted to be with Alice or Louis, her father. Then she was completely at ease: she laughed a lot and was very interactive. That was also pleasant for the parents, who got a lot back from their child. Sometimes it was also tiring, because Kiki could get very upset when she was tired or when Alice and Louis had something else to do. This became especially evident when Lothar, their second child, joined them. Alice remembers very well how Kiki always made friends at primary school, but that there was often some tension between her and her best friend at the time. Kiki could be very sad or angry when she was disappointed. For example, Alice remembers that one time she was not invited to a friend's birthday party. This upset her for two days. Alice felt that she exaggerated at such times.

Kiki found the transition to secondary school quite exciting. She was clever enough but was afraid she would not find any friends. Kiki also had her period in the first year. She was very ashamed of that. Alice felt that in the first year she began to struggle more and more with herself. She began to put on make-up, but also seemed to exaggerate in that respect. Alice sometimes thinks back nostalgically to the primary school years, when things were simpler. She can sometimes get annoyed with Kiki, who excludes her. And sometimes Kiki is downright rude. Then she can call Alice names and run away.

> In your professional or personal life, have you seen people change during puberty?

Teenagers change physically. They experience a growth spurt and become sexually mature. The hormones that are released during this period make adolescents temporarily less able to handle stress. They often react lightly, and their emotions sometimes run wild. Their brains change too. First the 'emotional' brain grows, and only later the areas at the front of the brain that help to inhibit, and where explicit mentalizing takes place. The connections between the different areas of the brain are re-established. If we look at Kiki, it could be that these changes have made the emotions, which she has always experienced intensely, even more intense and that Kiki does not yet have the mentalizing abilities to handle these emotions. Kiki does not just get sad when something happens between a best friend and her, she gets intensely sad. She cannot sufficiently control the intensity of her emotions herself, for example by putting the events that upset her into the right perspective. Bill, for his part, has perhaps always been a bit shy. That shyness now seems to have been magnified and replaced by shame.

These physical changes bring new opportunities and prepare adolescents to function independently in society, but they also come with great psychological challenges. Adolescents have to get a picture of who they are, where their talents lie, what goals they want to pursue in life and what education and job are appropriate. They have to detach themselves from home step by step, in order to eventually be able to stand on their own two feet. They have to trust that they can handle life without always falling back on parents or other caregivers. Adolescents must be able to be proud of themselves, proud of that changing body, without overestimating themselves. They have to learn to comply with agreements and rules that apply in society, for example in the classroom. They have to form relationships outside their own family, for example in a group of friends. 'Who am I?' and 'How do I relate to others?' are the two basic questions to which adolescents must find answers. These answers lay the foundation for the rest of their lives.

> How did you answer these questions for yourself during your adolescence? Do you have an image of who you are? Does your profession, for example, fit with how you see yourself? Which relationships are important to you? Have you developed relationships you are satisfied with?

Kiki struggles with these challenges. Maybe all the changes make her insecure, she feels alone. Maybe she wants to talk to her mother but gets annoyed when she overreacts. It may also play a part that Kiki now looks at her mother and her family differently than before. She can now better imagine that her home situation could have been different, that her mother and father could have been different parents. Past or recent events can take on a different meaning. In Bill's situation, it is quite possible that the impact of his parents' divorce and his father's immediate entry into a new relationship is experienced differently by him now than if it had occurred a few years earlier. Now Bill is more aware of it, perhaps more ashamed of it, and finds it strange that his father left his mother so soon, and even for such a young girl.

Adolescence also demands adjustments from parents: They have to be able to trust their child, let them go, without leaving them to their fate. In the example you can feel Alice struggling with this new relationship. She feels that Kiki is keeping her at a greater distance, but she also feels that Kiki has distanced herself too much, that she may not be able to cope with life as well as she would like.

Our society is attuned to these changes. Teenagers change schools at the start of puberty. In primary school, children usually spend years together, in a smaller school, and have a regular teacher. The group is small and familiar. Secondary schools are often larger, and adolescents usually end up in new classes with many other children they do not know. They often have different teachers who are sometimes better but also sometimes less attuned to them. So, they have to learn to deal with different social circumstances. Their school career is also increasingly focused on a profession or further education. Society gradually gives adolescents more legally defined freedoms and responsibilities. Their living environment is literally getting larger and is much more difficult for parents to oversee than when they were primary school children.

> Which of these changes or challenges did you struggle with as an adolescent? What effect did that have on your mood? If you have adolescents at home, what challenges do you see your child struggling with?

Vulnerable adolescents and the high P

It is therefore no coincidence that adolescence is the period in which many psychological problems arise. What is vulnerability and how do we recognize it?

Len and Violet

Len was born prematurely and has been a bit of a worry ever since. As a baby he was difficult to comfort, cried a lot, and did not sleep well. Particularly his fine motor skills were a bit behind, and he was almost two years old when he said his first words. In primary school he had learning difficulties, both with reading and with arithmetic. In addition, Len had several phobic fears, which could regularly upset him completely, and he was generally restless and agitated anyway. Fortunately, his parents were strong. They offered Len the necessary structure, safety, and regularity. They always discussed changes with him beforehand and kept the lines of communication with the school short. This enabled him to continue in mainstream education despite his vulnerability.

Violet has a history with a lot of burdening experiences. Her parents split up not long after her birth and she didn't have any contact with her father. She grew up with her mother, but she suddenly died of a heart attack, which Violet witnessed at the age of seven. Her father did not want to take care of her and because her grandparents were too old, she was placed in a foster family. The foster parents, who had several foster children in the house, became overburdened, so Violet was transferred to another family. Yet, Violet is doing well at school. She would like to become a nurse and works hard for school. She is loved in the classroom and has some friends. The foster service has often considered treatment for Violet because she has been through so much. However, she seems to be doing fine and has no obvious complaints.

Len and Violet are two completely different teenagers. Even though Len comes from a strong family, he is clearly more vulnerable than Violet, who has been through a lot, but always managed to pull through. Nor can Len's vulnerability be captured by a single label. There are cognitive problems, emotional disturbances, hyperactivity, and developmental delays. Perhaps there are also social and other problems. In psychiatry, it is customary to classify these problems. Len may have learning disabilities (dyscalculia, dyslexia), anxiety disorders (phobia), and developmental disabilities (autism spectrum disorder, ADHD). But does it help?

Recent studies show that such a division into all different diagnoses (the DSM-5, the best-known classification system, has more than 150!) is not very useful. After all, you often see that people who seek help have characteristics of different diagnoses. Someone who feels depressed is more likely to experience anxiety. Someone who is impulsive is also more likely to have behavioural problems. You can say: Those who are vulnerable have a greater chance of developing symptoms of various diagnoses. Len may be particularly vulnerable due to a predisposition and premature birth and therefore has a greatly increased risk of developing all kinds of psychological problems. In childhood, he may have learning difficulties and a developmental delay, as an adolescent he may have a lot of anxiety and compulsion, and as a young adult he may have psychotic or other serious symptoms. Compare it to intelligence. We are all more or less intelligent, and that intelligence will in the course of our lives express itself in capabilities and deficits in different areas, such as vocabulary, general knowledge, speed of processing, memory, spatial insight ... Those who are generally gifted, are often so in several of these areas, although this will express itself somewhat differently at different ages.

Recent studies precisely make this comparison between vulnerability to psychological problems and intelligence. Like intelligence, there may be a general measure of psychological problems, in this case vulnerability. A kind of IQ, but for psychological resilience or vulnerability. We call this the p-factor. The higher the p, the greater someone's vulnerability to developing psychological problems. The p-factor in fact means that we do not develop a psychological disorder just like that or in isolation from other problems. It is the expression of a greater or lesser vulnerability. Some people will be very vulnerable and therefore often exhibit psychological problems throughout their lives. Other people will have great psychological resilience. Of course, they too can be tested by life, but in general they will be able to handle more negative life events or changes without becoming unbalanced.

In the example you can see that Len has a high p: He may be genetically and biologically strained and can experience a lot of psychological symptoms with the slightest change or stress in his life. For Len, puberty can be a real stumbling block. Fortunately, his parents have a good sense of this and offer him the structure, safety, and support that can help him to continue to develop as well as possible. Violet, in turn, is very resilient. She has had a lot to cope with, but she keeps her goal of becoming a nurse in mind, can continue with her tasks (e.g., going to school) and has good relationships with her peers.

Puberty is an additional challenge for vulnerable adolescents. Adolescence involves so many changes and challenges that even minimal psychological vulnerability can cause symptoms. For example, studies show that between 10 and 25 per cent of adolescents have self-harmed or had thoughts of death. Precisely because of the hormonal and neural changes, symptoms in young people often manifest themselves first in mood swings and impulsiveness. You could say that these symptoms are the quickest indicators of vulnerability, but they do not necessarily indicate serious vulnerability.

Girls and boys will often develop slightly different symptoms. For example, girls are more likely to develop symptoms of emotional disorders, such as anxiety, depression, or eating problems, while boys are more likely to have symptoms of behavioural disorders. As the severity of the vulnerability (p) increases, both boys and girls often develop symptoms of different disorders, both emotional and behavioural.

Do you know examples of young people and adults in your surroundings who are very mentally vulnerable (p)? How would you estimate this for yourself?

What do you think makes people more or less vulnerable? How could you relate this to what you have read in this book?

Attachment, mentalizing, and epistemic trust

Let us review the three interrelated basic themes we have discussed in this book (i.e., attachment, mentalizing, and epistemic trust) and link them to resilience and vulnerability. In addition to biological factors, the experiences that people have in the early years of their lives naturally influence their vulnerability. Back to Sophia, whom we gave as an example in Chapter 5.

Sophia and Patty
Sophia is Patty's daughter, who was emotionally neglected and sexually abused as a child. As a child, Sophia experiences a lot of insecurity in her contact with Patty. She cannot trust Patty to be available. Moreover, Patty is unpredictable, so that Sophia often does not know what to expect. She has a disorganized attachment style. Sophia's basic feeling is probably 'insecurity'. She shuts herself off from her surroundings. Maybe she wants to trust a nice teacher, but she doesn't dare. She grows up with the image that she is a worthless child. She tries to assess and predict her mother's moods, so that she does nothing to upset Patty. She keeps her own 'mess' inside. She has never had the experience that others could help her with what she feels. She doesn't know how to handle it herself either. Sophia tries to put her emotions away, not to feel them. She keeps her distance from others. During puberty it becomes increasingly difficult to keep herself in balance. She often drinks alcohol alone in her room, to numb all her emotions. She self-harms almost every night. When a boy showed interest in her recently, she went to bed with him. For a moment she felt loved, but afterwards she only felt more miserable. She often thinks about suicide.

Let's also follow Violet, the girl who has been through so much already.

Violet
Violet is often sad when she thinks about her mum. They had a good time together. Her mother often talked about her father and why they had not stayed together. Yet, she was never accusing. Grandad and grandma often visited and Violet had a good relationship with them. After her mother's death, grandma often talked about her. At that time, Violet had a nice class. It was nice that school continued as usual. When she was older, Violet went through a difficult period. She was very angry with her mother for not being there anymore. Why could she not just have parents who helped her, like other children? Fortunately, in the foster home where she now lives, the parents realized that things were not going well with Violet. They listened to her anger. Violet then quickly started to cry because she felt how much she missed her mother. She told her foster mother that she liked being with them, but at the same time, she was afraid that she would have to leave again. Her foster mother said that she understood that and that she too could not promise that nothing would ever happen to them, but that she was very happy now that they could talk about it together in this way.

Before reading on, think about both examples. How do you think the two girls differ?

In these examples, we can get into the minds of Sophia and Violet. We can see why Sophia is vulnerable and Violet resilient, why Sophia runs the risk of developing all kinds of psychological problems and Violet is much stronger. We feel how unsafe the world is for Sophia, both her inner world and her outer world. Sophia has a disorganized attachment and is epistemically very distrustful. She does not dare to connect with others and she does not dare to connect with her own emotions. Sophia cannot mentalize properly about herself or the other person. She quickly enters pre-mentalizing modes. Sometimes she is in a pretend mode, in which she can feel empty or flattened. Often, however, she is in a psychic equivalence mode. She is worthless. Others cannot be trusted. She doesn't dare to accept anything from others. Everything confirms the convictions she already had about herself, others, and the world. Sophia shuts herself off from others and no longer learns from her social surroundings. She rigidly sticks to what she knows: Her convictions about herself, the other, and the world, her way of dealing with herself and with her emotions, her pattern of interaction with others . . . Sophia has managed to survive the unpredictability in the contact with Patty but has shielded herself from the outside world in such a way that she no longer has room to learn and to change.

Violet, on the other hand, is rather securely attached. She may lose her mentalizing ability, for example when she thinks about her mother, but recovers more quickly and has more epistemic trust. Therefore, in this example, she is open to her foster mother and what she learns about herself, her mother, and their mutual relationship. She dares to experience her feelings and she lets her foster mother think along with her. She can then feel how afraid she is of losing these foster parents as well, but she realizes that this is only a fear. They *are* not gone. She can talk to her foster mother about this fear, which helps her to put it back into perspective. She can talk about her anger, which helps her to realize that she is also missing her mother. This helps Violet to move on again. Unlike Sophia, Violet has not closed herself off and remains open. She is still learning, she remains flexible. This creates space to look at the things that have happened differently. She is not stuck on the idea that everyone will eventually abandon her. Yes, that is a fear, but by talking about it with her foster mother, it remains just that, and it does not become an unchangeable truth in her head.

Rigidity is the hallmark of vulnerability, and flexibility is the hallmark of resilience. Those who have enough flexibility to adapt to unpleasant life events (such as a divorce from parents) or to changes and challenges that development confronts you with (such as puberty), will be stronger. In contrast, mentally vulnerable people are often rigid. For example, they may cling to certain beliefs ('Spiders are dangerous', 'People take advantage of you when you are vulnerable'). They also often experience everything that happens to them from the same frame of reference ('You see, he looks at me in a strange way, as if he does not believe me'). Furthermore, they often react in the same way (e.g., they always attack when they are criticized) or quickly feel the same emotions (e.g., they always get anxious when their partner comes home late).

Rigidity means that you no longer learn from experience: Even if this dog turns out not to be dangerous, this experience does not generalize to other dogs. Even if your partner has always proved trustworthy, you continue to distrust him or her. Rigidity is often maintained by epistemic distrust: You dare not trust that the other is someone you can learn from. And so, you shut yourself up in your own truth, in the way you have always experienced yourself, the world and the people around you, and the way you have always thought about others. Through epistemic distrust, not much can change in your ideas, in your truth.

That completes the puzzle. If you have a sufficiently secure attachment, you dare to trust yourself and others. Therefore, you are closer to yourself and your own needs and you are better attuned to the other, which means that you mentalize better. Because of this, you recognize the good and less good intentions of others better and can therefore experience epistemic trust towards others when their intentions are good and you can learn something from them, but you can also suspend that epistemic trust and remain vigilant when the other person is not so trustworthy after all. Secure attachment, mentalizing, and epistemic trust lay the foundations for flexibility: you are open to new knowledge, learning experiences, and insights that others share with you, which enables you to adapt well to challenging life circumstances. If, on the other hand, you have an insecure attachment, you often do not trust yourself or others enough. You mentalize less well about yourself and others, and can be overwhelmed by the intensity of emotions, or you become detached from your own emotions and needs. You fill in too much for others, which can make you suspicious of others' intentions. As a result, you may become epistemically distrustful or hypervigilant, and stop accepting anything from others. The result is that you remain stuck in your own rigid ways of thinking, feeling, and experiencing.

Perhaps you need to let this sink in for a moment. It is the core of all the theory in this book. It brings together how we think about resilience, parenting, and development. We make children more resilient when we support them to learn (again) from reliable others, so that they can adapt flexibly, even when life is difficult. We do this by making contact, installing safety, and helping them to mentalize better about themselves and others. Because, even though the foundations are fragile, not all is lost. Not even for Sophia.

Strengthening resilience in adolescence

Problems in attachment, mentalizing, and epistemic trust will be amplified in adolescence by all the challenges and changes. You could see this in Sophia: She has always been disorganized in her attachment and may have always had a lot of epistemic distrust, but it is only when she changes physically, becomes more aware of her identity, and has to form close relationships outside the family, that she becomes completely overwhelmed.

Earlier, we wrote that adolescents face two major questions: 'Who am I?' and 'How do I connect with others?' For children with a foundation of insecure attachment and a lack of epistemic trust, these are difficult to resolve. Youngsters who are anxiously attached may become too anxious when they have to stand on their own two feet. They continue to cling to their parents and fail to change that relationship. Or, they cling to their peers. They lack the self-confidence to make their own identity choices. Avoidantly attached children may stand on their own two feet too much, become elusive for their parents, and no longer allow themselves to be guided. They have too little trust in others to allow them to take over the steering wheel in a phase in which they do not yet have an overview of everything.

What can we do to make children more resilient in this life period, which is difficult for some? In fact, it boils down to the following:

- Think about the child even more consciously than before.
- Make conscious contact with him or her.
- Help him or her to mentalize better.

Let's see how that worked out for Kiki and Bill.

Alice and Kiki
Alice feels that something is going on with Kiki. How can she talk to Kiki about it? After all, Kiki is keeping her at a distance. This also means that Alice avoids talking about it. We can think with Alice about the experiences behind Kiki's behaviour (mentalizing). She may be ashamed of her mother. She was always

such a nice child—her mother still repeats this regularly—and now she feels anything but nice at home. Maybe she feels like a burden? Or is she afraid that Alice will overreact? Or that she will immediately say that she needs treatment, while Kiki herself is already scared that she may be a bit weird? Alice could talk to Louis, and together they could think about Kiki's mental state and their own, and about a good approach to the conversation. Louis may have different ideas about this than Alice, which may help her to discover new angles. They can think about which of them is best to talk to Kiki. Perhaps Alice, who has always been closer to Kiki, but who can also tend to overreact emotionally for that very reason? Or Louis, who doesn't care as much when Kiki reacts in a distant way and who may also be a little less emotionally charged for Kiki? They can think about how difficult or exciting they find it to start that conversation and how quickly they might become emotional or agitated themselves. They can think about how they want to approach Kiki and what the possible effect on Kiki will be if they do it this way or that. And they can think about what they want to say to her.

Lex and Bill
In turn, Lex could ask colleagues whether they have noticed the changes in Bill and if they have any ideas about how he is doing. This might include not only hypothesizing that Bill is having a hard time dealing with the divorce, but also what effect this (and other things) is having on how Bill feels about being alone at school. Lex might hypothesize that Bill is very insecure, lonely, and sad. That he might like to fit in with the class but is too insecure and self-conscious to take the initiative. He might consider the effect on Bill if he were to discuss this with him on a one-to-one basis. If Bill initially brushes him off, it could also be an expression of his insecurity and shame, rather than of the fact that he really doesn't want to be contacted about this. Lex doesn't know all this for sure, but he's trying to make sense of it.

The first thing parents, teachers, or other supervisors can do is to mentalize: about themselves and about the adolescent. It can be useful to involve your team: colleagues, friends, partner . . . You can't be sure of anything, of course, but thinking about your child and looking at his or her behaviour with fresh eyes can help you to attune better. Think back to the chapter on attachment: attunement is better when you are able to mirror congruent (fitting or connecting) and marked (well-regulated). This also requires that you understand and can handle your own emotions evoked in the contact well enough.

Take a recent example of your own child, a pupil, or a client. Take a moment to consciously consider what might have been going on in his or her mind at that moment, what effect that might have had on you, and what it would have been like for this child and for you to engage in conversation about it.

When you engage in conversation, show your commitment. You can use ostensive cues for this: You go to your child's room, look at him or her, make time, call his or her name. This shows them: 'This is important. I think you are important. I think what you feel and experience is important.' Ostensive cues form the base for establishing contact; think back to the experiment we discussed in Chapter 6, in which toddlers had to choose between two objects.

Alice and Louis decide that Louis will talk to Kiki. He chooses a moment when Kiki is in her room and has no schoolwork to do. After knocking on her door, he goes inside. 'Kiki, I'd really like to talk to you', says Louis, looking at her and sitting down on the bed. Kiki feels: Dad is serious.

Making real contact is sometimes tensive. Do you really dare to say to a pupil or client: You matter?

When the foundation to establish contact is there, you can ask questions. The best way to find out what moves your child and to help them understand themselves and their emotions is to ask open questions. Above all, help your child to get a grip on him/herself. You can tell your child what is going on or why he is reacting the way he is, or you can reassure him repeatedly or solve his problems for him, but this will not help him in the long run. What matters is that your child starts to understand itself. What they feel means something.

Once you know better what is going on, you can mirror more congruently, for example by showing how you understand your child. This will stimulate your child's mentalizing and he or she will be able to understand his or her own confusing feelings better. Think of the baby who only experiences discomfort and needs a parent to understand and handle that tension. Because of all the changes, the emotions of adolescents are also sometimes mostly unrest and tension. Slowing down and pausing can help your child to get a better grip on it. It also helps you to understand your child better. This will also make it easier to adapt to his or her mental state. An adolescent who feels that the other person is really making an effort to understand him or her and who feels seen and acknowledged in what he or she feels, will feel safer. Together, attunement and safety create epistemic trust: If your child experiences that you really understand him or her from the inside, then they are much more likely to let you help them think about the issues they are struggling with.

Lex went to see Bill after class. Bill, I would like to talk to you. Lex mentions his observation: 'I have the impression that you are on your own a bit more often. I wanted to see how you are doing.' Bill is startled by Lex's question. He had hoped that no one would notice. 'I'm fine, no problem,' he says quickly. Lex hesitates for a moment: Should he leave Bill alone or ask him more questions? He notices that he doesn't really believe Bill when he says that everything is okay. 'Bill, I would like to believe you, but I find myself doubting whether everything is all right. You may find it an awkward question, but I genuinely wonder how you are doing. I've seen you change over the past year and sometimes I think I can sense that you're less cheerful than before.' Bill has mixed feelings about this. On the one hand he's glad Lex is talking to him, but on the other hand the last thing he wants is for it to become a thing. 'I'm fine. I don't need anything special.' Lex notices some hesitation when Bill says this. 'You know Bill, I wasn't planning on doing anything in particular. I just wanted to talk to you.'

This reassures Bill that Lex doesn't immediately want to call his mother or treat him as a serious problem. He opens up a little more: 'It's just different than last year.' Lex responds in an attuned way. 'Yes, I think I can see that too. What's different?' He feels he shouldn't ask too many more questions and should follow up on Bill's opening. Bill cautiously begins to say more: 'I just don't know anymore. Last year everything seemed to go effortlessly. Now everything is so disappointing.' 'What are you so disappointed about?' Bill continues: 'I feel less at home in my class. Marco has changed classes and I'm not sure who I can hang out with now.' Lex mirrors slightly, 'It seems annoying to you that you don't feel so much at home in your class.' Bill continues: 'I also find it hard to approach the others in the class. They don't seem to need me.' Bill reflects: 'I understand that you may be more insecure about making new contacts. I don't know if they don't want you around, but if you feel that way, it might make you more insecure.'

Lex and Bill continue their conversation. Bill notices that it feels good to talk about what's bothering him. He likes the fact that Lex doesn't immediately come up with solutions, such as putting him next to someone in the classroom who can then 'become a friend'. He also felt no judgement from Lex. Lex's doubts about whether his classmates really dislike him also made him think a little. When Bill sits next to Thomas in class the next day, he looks at him. Bill looks back and smiles.

Lex tries to make space so that it becomes safe for Bill to say something. He tries to attune to Bill's mental state. When he thinks he can, he supports Bill by mirroring him. He takes a poorly mentalized statement from Bill ('They don't want me') seriously, but without going along with it. The aim is not for Lex to 'know' what is going on with Bill at the end of their conversation. The aim is that he makes contact, seeks to connect with Bill and creates something of an openness in Bill that allows him to be more flexible. In contact with Lex, Bill may experience that, at least, not everyone dislikes him. Lex plants a very small seed, which may cause Bill to be a little different in class in the hour after this conversation.

Perhaps you can already feel the tension in such a conversation. How quickly will Bill think that Lex is going to make an issue of it (read: embarrass him). And how quickly will Kiki look for something negative behind Louis' visit to her room: Have I done something wrong? Why are you meddling with me? Are you disappointed in me? These are all signs that they mentalize less well under stress. Adolescents often go to great lengths to interpret the intentions of others, such as their parents or teachers. It is therefore important to be transparent and to 'subtitle' yourself sufficiently.

Louis notices that Kiki is surprised that he sits on her bed like this. He clarifies himself: 'I can imagine you're surprised that I'm sitting here and not Mum. We talked about it together and we thought it would be easier if I talked to you. You may wonder why we want to talk to you. Well, we are worried, and we find it hard to have a sense of how you are doing. I'm here because I think it's really important to know better what's going on.'

Resilience reinforces itself

Teachers, social workers, and perhaps parents too, may wonder what difference they can make. Perhaps Sophia's teacher feels how massive Sophia's burden is and knows how many problems her mother Patty has. How useful then is it to do what we have been promoting here for a whole book: Mentalize, (re-) connect and generate epistemic trust? Let's be clear about this: it's extremely valuable. One teacher, one caregiver can make a difference, even with extremely vulnerable children. Research shows that adults who can name one support figure from their childhood—a grandmother, an aunt, neighbour, teacher—on average have a better outcome after treatment than people who lacked such a person.

Let's go back to Lex and Bill for a moment. At the end of the example, something happened that shows the effect of the conversation. Lex 'opened up' to Bill. Bill, who usually assumes that his classmates are not waiting for him, was momentarily thrown into doubt and experienced that, in any case, Lex was waiting for him. Something of an epistemic trust comes into being, which we see work its way into his first contact afterwards: Bill experiences the contact with the gaze of his classmate slightly differently than before. He is less rigid and looks at the world around him with slightly different eyes. Perhaps he answers the gaze a little differently this time. He may smile a little, which in turn may make his classmate feel something of contact. And so, a seed has been planted in Lex's conversation that triggers something different in Bill's contacts.

We call this process salutogenesis, the strengthening of healthy developments, which creates a positive spiral. By really engaging with Bill as a teacher, Lex begins such a process. He creates an opening that influences other contacts. In these other contacts, Bill can really start to change. He can become more receptive to the goodness of his classmates and respond to them more adequately instead of letting contact with them slip away from him in a state of epistemic hypervigilance. It 'connects' just a little bit differently between Bill and Thomas, and Bill can build on that. Through these interactions Bill will eventually be able to experience himself and the world differently again. This is the core of recovery.

Of course, the foundation of Bill is more solid than that of Sophia. Sophia may need a treatment in which systematic and structured work is done on the recovery of her mentalizing and epistemic trust. Moreover, her mother Patty will also need help: If she remains unpredictable and disturbed, it is questionable whether it will help Sophia to open up at home. She might be damaged further.

One of the reasons why we wanted to write this book is that we are convinced that parents, teachers, and social workers can mean a lot to children when they make real contact from a basic mentalizing attitude. Each of us can give a child, an adolescent, a neighbour, or a colleague the feeling that they are being mentalized, which creates space to be open to the other. Not only for the other who plants this seed, but for many more people. This openness to learn from others is the greatest asset we can give people to make them resilient.

> Which child do you really want to connect with this week? How will you do that?

Summary

In this chapter, we discussed how the changes in puberty can test vulnerable adolescents. This led us to the recent concept of the p-factor as a measure of a person's vulnerability to developing mental health problems. We have also linked this vulnerability to the basic themes of this book: attachment, mentalizing, and epistemic trust. Securely attached children who feel mentalized will themselves mentalize better and be more open to reliable information from others (epistemic trust), which will make them flexible and resilient. The chance that they will develop psychological problems is therefore smaller. Conversely, insecurely attached children will often mentalize less well about themselves and others and will be more epistemically distrustful or even hypervigilant. This can give rise to rigidity, so that they remain stuck in non-helpful patterns in emotions, thoughts, behaviour, and relationships. And that often makes them vulnerable to psychopathology.

The main point we have tried to make in this chapter is that each of us can make a difference. If we want to strengthen the resilience of children and adolescents, the most important thing is to make real contact. To create a contact that plants a seed from which this child, this adolescent or this adult can once again be open to the good in this world and allow themselves to be helped in the confrontation with all the challenges life throws at us.

Epilogue

When we started writing this book, our plan was to make the rich theories surrounding attachment, mentalizing, and epistemic trust as accessible as possible. We hoped that not only psychotherapists would benefit from it, but also parents, teachers, and other caregivers. In addition, mentalizing theory has developed rapidly in recent years and concepts such as epistemic trust have not yet found their way into practice, even among clinicians. While writing the book, the plan became more of a mission. We became more and more convinced that there is indeed a world to be gained if these theories find more acceptance outside the clinical field. We believe that education, upbringing, and the broad range of care benefits from a better understanding of these theories.

We all know a student, neighbour, client, or adolescent who feels alone and misunderstood. Maybe we see it—like many others—but hesitate to really connect and mean something to them. Or we think it won't make a difference after all. Let this be a message from this book: everyone can make a difference. Making someone feel important, mentalizing about someone, connecting with someone who may not have felt contact for a long time does make a difference. And maybe more than you think. If you are the teacher who sees and understands a child beyond his or her annoying behaviour, you might be the first to restore something of damaged epistemic trust. If you are the general practitioner who can see and reach the grumpy teenager during a consultation, you might start a process of salutogenesis. Then you open up something that was previously closed and no longer allowed to change. Then you plant in this child or adult the seed that will allow it to blossom.

Recommended reading

Literature

This book has no formal scientific references to keep it accessible for all readers. Interested readers may find more background in (among much other literature) these books and papers:

Allen, J. G., & Fonagy, P. (2006). *Handbook of Mentalization-Based Treatment*. Chichester: John Wiley.

Allen, J. G., Fonagy, P., & Bateman, A. W. (2008). *Mentalizing in Clinical Practice*. Arlington: American Psychiatric Publishing.

Bateman, A., & Fonagy, P. (2004). *Psychotherapy for Borderline Personality Disorder: Mentalization Based Treatment*. Oxford: Oxford University Press.

Bateman, A. W., & Fonagy, P. (2006). *Mentalization Based Treatment for Borderline Personality Disorder: A Practical Guide*. Oxford: Oxford University Press.

Bateman, A., & Fonagy, P. (2012). *Handbook of Mentalizing in Mental Health Practice*. Washington, DC: American Psychiatric Publishing.

Bateman, A. W., & Fonagy, P. (2016). *Mentalization Based Treatment for Personality Disorders: A Practical Guide*. Oxford: Oxford University Press.

Bateman, A., Fonagy, P., Campbell, C., Luyten, P. & Debbané, M. (2023). *Cambridge Guide to Mentalization-Based Treatment (MBT)*. Cambridge: Cambridge University Press.

Fonagy, P., Luyten, P., Allison, E., & Campbell, C. (2017). What we have changed our minds about: Part 1. Borderline personality disorder as a limitation of resilience. *Borderline personality disorder and emotion dysregulation, 4*, 11. https://doi.org/10.1186/s40479-017-0061-9

Fonagy, P., Luyten, P., Allison, E., & Campbell, C. (2017). What we have changed our minds about: Part 2. Borderline personality disorder, epistemic trust and the developmental significance of social communication. *Borderline personality disorder and emotion dysregulation, 4*, 9. https://doi.org/10.1186/s40479-017-0062-8

Fonagy, P., Luyten, P., Allison, E., & Campbell, C. (2019). Mentalizing, Epistemic Trust and the Phenomenology of Psychotherapy. *Psychopathology, 52*(2), 94–103. https://doi.org/10.1159/000501526

Luyten, P., Campbell, C., Allison, E., & Fonagy, P. (2020). The Mentalizing Approach to Psychopathology: State of the Art and Future Directions. *Annual review of clinical psychology, 16*, 297–325. https://doi.org/10.1146/annurev-clinpsy-071919-015355

Sharp, C., & Bevington, D. (2022). *Mentalizing in Psychotherapy. A Guide for Practitioners*. Guilford Publications, Inc.

Index

For the benefit of digital users, indexed terms that span two pages (e.g., 52–53) may, on occasion, appear on only one of those pages.